I0820465

CANNABIS

Edible

Series Editor: Andrew F. Smith

EDIBLE is a revolutionary series of books dedicated to food and drink that explores the rich history of cuisine. Each book reveals the global history and culture of one type of food or beverage.

Already published

Apple Erika Janik, *Avocado* Jeff Miller, *Banana* Lorna Piatti-Farnell, *Barbecue* Jonathan Deutsch and Megan J. Elias, *Beans* Nathalie Rachel Morris, *Beef* Lorna Piatti-Farnell, *Beer* Gavin D. Smith, *Berries* Heather Arndt Anderson, *Biscuits and Cookies* Anastasia Edwards, *Brandy* Becky Sue Epstein, *Bread* William Rubel, *Breakfast Cereal* Kathryn Cornell Dolan, *Cabbage* Meg Muckenhoupt, *Cake* Nicola Humble, *Cannabis* Bradley J. Borougerdi, *Caviar* Nichola Fletcher, *Champagne* Becky Sue Epstein, *Cheese* Andrew Dalby, *Chillies* Heather Arndt Anderson, *Chocolate* Sarah Moss and Alexander Badenoch, *Cocktails* Joseph M. Carlin, *Coconut* Constance L. Kirker and Mary Newman, *Cod* Elisabeth Townsend, *Coffee* Jonathan Morris, *Corn* Michael Owen Jones, *Curry* Colleen Taylor Sen, *Dates* Nawal Nasrallah, *Doughnut* Heather Delancey Hunwick, *Dumplings* Barbara Gallani, *Edible Flowers* Constance L. Kirker and Mary Newman, *Edible Insects* Gina Louise Hunter, *Eggs* Diane Toops, *Fats* Michelle Phillipov, *Figs* David C. Sutton, *Foie Gras* Norman Kolpas, *Game* Paula Young Lee, *Gin* Lesley Jacobs Solmonson, *Hamburger* Andrew F. Smith, *Herbs* Gary Allen, *Herring* Kathy Hunt, *Honey* Lucy M. Long, *Hot Dog* Bruce Kraig, *Hummus* Harriet Nussbaum, *Ice Cream* Laura B. Weiss, *Jam, Jelly and Marmalade* Sarah B. Hood, *Lamb* Brian Yarvin, *Lemon* Toby Sonneman, *Liqueur* Lesley Jacobs Solmonson, *Lobster* Elisabeth Townsend, *Mango* Constance L. Kirker and Mary Newman, *Melon* Sylvia Lovegren, *Milk* Hannah Velten, *Moonshine* Kevin R. Kosar, *Mushroom* Cynthia D. Bertelsen, *Mustard* Demet Güzey, *Nuts* Ken Albala, *Offal* Nina Edwards, *Olive* Fabrizia Lanza, *Onions and Garlic* Martha Jay, *Oranges* Clarissa Hyman, *Oyster* Carolyn Tillie, *Pancake* Ken Albala, *Pasta and Noodles* Kantha Shelke, *Pickles* Jan Davison, *Pie* Janet Clarkson, *Pineapple* Kaori O'Connor, *Pizza* Carol Helstosky, *Pomegranate* Damien Stone, *Pork* Katharine M. Rogers, *Potato* Andrew F. Smith, *Pudding* Jeri Quinzio, *Rice* Renee Marton, *Rum* Richard Foss, *Saffron* Ramin Ganeshram, *Salad* Judith Weinraub, *Salmon* Nicolaas Mink, *Sandwich* Bee Wilson, *Sauces* Maryann Tebben, *Sausage* Gary Allen, *Seaweed* Kaori O'Connor, *Shrimp* Yvette Florio Lane, *Soda and Fizzy Drinks* Judith Levin, *Soup* Janet Clarkson, *Spices* Fred Czarra, *SPAM* Kelly A. Spring, *Sweets and Candy* Laura Mason, *Tea* Helen Saberi, *Tequila* Ian Williams, *Tomato* Clarissa Hyman, *Truffle* Zachary Nowak, *Vanilla* Rosa Abreu-Runkel, *Vodka* Patricia Herlihy, *Water* Ian Miller, *Whiskey* Kevin R. Kosar, *Wine* Marc Millon, *Yoghurt* June Hersh

Cannabis

A Global History

Bradley J. Borougerdi

REAKTION BOOKS

To the students who've studied cannabis history with me in my world civilizations course over the last decade. Your engaging discussions and thought-provoking enquiries were indispensable.

Published by Reaktion Books Ltd
Unit 32, Waterside
44–48 Wharf Road
London N1 7UX, UK
www.reaktionbooks.co.uk

First published 2025

Printed and bound in India by Replika Press Pvt. Ltd

A catalogue record for this book is available from the British Library

ISBN 978 1 83639 007 7

Contents

Introduction

Cannabis is a global plant. It can survive almost anywhere above near-freezing temperatures. Human consumption of it has a long and complicated history, filled with complex different meanings across multiple societies. Chinese peasants ate cannabis seeds as a staple. Southeast Asians have drunk concoctions of its leaves for centuries. Persians popularly associated preparations of it with Sufi *dervishes*, while legend claims that Siddhartha Gautama survived by eating just one cannabis seed per day for six years. In Uzbekistan a traditional food called *guc'kand* combines cannabis leaves and flowers with a variety of ingredients. Cultures from the continent of Africa initiated the concept of smoking cannabis, while Europeans were the first to carry it across the Atlantic as a fibre, stimulating its dispersal across the Americas. Most societies have made some variety of oil, medicine and fibrous products out of the plant, and ingesting it has become a culturally significant custom for many people around the world.

Despite its diverse, multi-purpose application, however, the most popular association with cannabis – at least since the mid-twentieth century – has been as a smokable substance. Its leaf has become an iconic symbol for consumers all over the world. The plant is still criminalized in most countries, but many have been grappling with what forms of consumption, if any, should be allowed. By the 2010s recreational markets began popping up in areas where cannabis had previously been illegal, spurring numerous innovations in the way people eat and drink it. Fizzy drinks, teas, tonics, sweets, baked goods and full-course meals infused with various parts of the plant are bought and sold by millions of people every day now. This book connects various historical pathways of cannabis consumption into a global narrative to describe how the world developed a taste for this multidimensional plant.

Cannabis sativa leaf.

Jean Bourdichon, female and male cannabis plants, miniatures from a book of hours, *c.* 1505–8. One of the earliest European depictions of cannabis, the labelling of the plants is opposite to how they are recognized today.

Human relationships with the plant go back a long time, but the historical seeds of cannabis's transformation into a global food and drink were sown in the early modern era (1500s–1600s CE). This is a vital period for cannabis history because different cannabis cultures started encountering each other more frequently, creating an entangled history of consumption that is multilayered and complex. From here, we see how the plant came to the Americas and dispersed across the continents, and how cultural clashes between different uses invested it with exotic meanings that contributed to its transformation into the most widely used illegal substance in the world. Along the way, Europeans tried to tame what they considered an 'Oriental' variety into something beneficial for Westernized medicine. Meanwhile, its use as an industrial commodity waxed and waned, with advocates fighting against the rising stigmas associated with its subversive uses.

Something similar occurred in the United States, where a culture war sprang up around cannabis that pitted consumption patterns against each other while cannabis itself became a transnational symbol of countercultural identity. This counterculturalism sparked a resurgence in the popularity of eating and drinking preparations of the plant, which gave way to the commercial evolution of cannabis-infused foods, drinks and edibles that dominate headlines today. In Amsterdam the Dutch developed an epicentre of drug tourism with hundreds of 'coffee shops' that have operated as 'grey area' businesses for decades. In the UK, where consumption and control were intricately tied to the history of British imperialism, cannabis has evolved into a quasi-acceptable recreational drug for subcultures in British society. African, Asian and Amerindian cultures have had their own complicated yet evolving relationships with it as well, making it one of the most controversial worldly plants known to man.

I
What Is Cannabis?

> [It is] grown both legally and illegally all over the world,
> wild or cultivated, for utilitarian or intoxicant use,
> from Calcutta to Beacon Hill.
>
> Lester Grinspoon, *Marihuana Reconsidered* (1971)

Cannabis is a dioecious species, which means that its male and female reproductive organs grow on separate plants. Some varieties can express hermaphroditic characteristics, but for the most part, female cannabis plants produce flowers that are coated with a sticky resin, whereas the males produce a dusty form of pollen. This pollen sticks to the resinous secretion of the female flowers, which then form into clusters of flowering pods where the seeds develop. Dozens of seeds can grow within a single flowering cluster on a female plant, with each reflecting a unique combination of the genetic code it inherited from the parent plants.

There is a complicated history behind the question of how many different cannabis species there are. The debate has yet to be settled, but many today identify *Cannabis sativa*, *Cannabis indica* and *Cannabis ruderalis* as separate species distinguishable by phenotypical characteristics such as size and leaf shape, or at the molecular level by their cannabinoid content. More recently, legislative practices have defined hemp as cannabis

Inflorescence and parts of *Cannabis sativa*, 19th century, engraving. The left side represents the female flowering parts, while the right side reflects the male equivalent.

that contains less than .03 per cent tetrahydrocannabinol (THC) – the plant's primary psychoactive cannabinoid – but *Cannabis sativa* has often been used historically to define these non-psychoactive cultivars as well. However, each plant also contains more than a hundred other cannabinoids within its molecular structure, and there are no reproductive barriers between species. This means there are endless possibilities for creating different strains or cultivars with unique expressions of aroma, taste and the pharmacological texture of effects that users describe as a 'high', which is why it is so difficult to standardize the experience of cannabis consumption.

It is also why a trip to a cannabis dispensary usually results in a flood of options with eccentric names, such as Purple Urkle, Afgooey, Durban Poison, White Rhino, African Black Magic, Ice Cream Cake, Do-Si-Dos, Gorilla Cookies, AK-47, Big Buddha Cheese, Buddha Kush, Fruity Pebbles, Lava Cake, Sweet Island Skunk, Gelato Runtz and Miracle Alien Cookies. That's just a small sample from the hundreds available out there to choose from, which can be a daunting task even for experienced users. 'Budtenders' at dispensaries and online resources such as Weedmaps and Leafly can aid people in navigating through some of the uncertainty, but new varieties pop up all the time.

The dizzying nomenclature behind different cannabis strains is not the only source of confusion, either. There is also the issue of what to call the plant. Despite references to it more generally as 'marijuana', I use that word more specifically when referring to the dried, female inflorescences that contain levels of THC strong enough to produce mind-altering effects, along with any baked goods, infused drinks and medicinal tinctures that contain extracts of these flowering parts. They are often colloquially referred to as 'buds'. 'Ganja' is another common term for these buds, but it has been used in some circumstances to describe the entire plant as well. Moreover, I sometimes use 'cannabis' and 'hemp' interchangeably, but there is a difference. Cannabis, for example, more broadly describes all varieties of the plant, whereas hemp is used specifically in reference to varieties with little to no THC content. All hemp is cannabis, in other words, but not all cannabis is hemp. There is an exception, however, such as the phrase 'Indian hemp' being used in historical sources to denote psychoactive preparations of cannabis.

Human selection has shaped the evolution of cannabis genetics. Those who valued its fibre chose different characteristics for reproduction than those who prized the plant's psychoactive properties. Nevertheless, all species contain parts that are viable for human consumption.

The Edible Parts

The human–cannabis connection seems to be as old as just about any people–plant relationship in history. Exactly when it began is hard to say, but archaeological evidence points to Asia as the earliest continent to develop a culture of consumption. If nourishment had anything to do with why people were first attracted to the plant, then its seeds would have certainly been considered the most valuable part. After all, they contain high concentrations of proteins, carbohydrates and beneficial fats such as omega-3 and omega-6 that help sustain a healthy diet. They are also small and contain a variety of valuable trace minerals. Of course, harvesting the seeds would have brought people directly into contact with the potentially psychoactive secretion that covers the outer portion of the seed pods on ripening female plants, but it is difficult to determine how long it would have taken people to recognize the medicinal value of that resin.

At some point, eating cannabis seeds – also referred to as hempseed – became somewhat customary in parts of Asia. A renowned herbalist from the Ming dynasty (1368–1644) named Li Shizhen discussed their consumption as both a food and a medicine in a manuscript that took him decades to compile. Published posthumously in 1596 CE, it contains a section that reflects how the seed had already developed a well-established reputation, for he cited manuscripts with descriptions of its use going back centuries. Among others, he described a porridge-like substance that produced a calming effect when ingested. Versions of this dish are still consumed in China today.[1]

Persians have also used cannabis seeds as a food and medicine for thousands of years. Some even claim that the Farsi word *shah'daneh* – which translates as 'king of seeds' – is a reference to cannabis, although others suggest it refers to

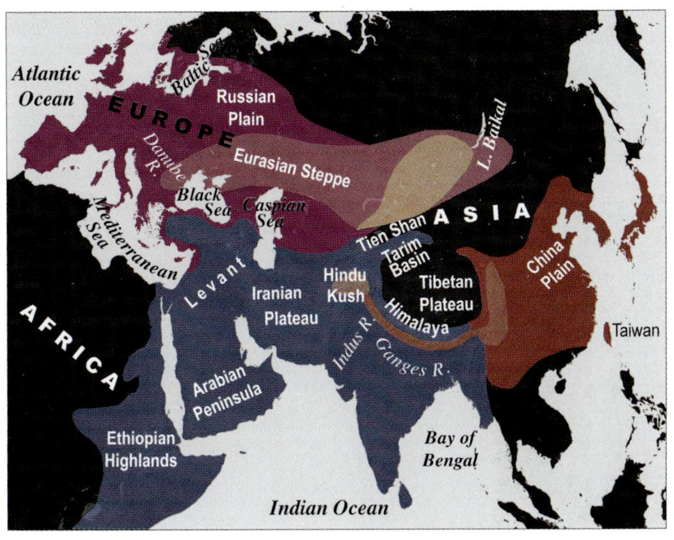

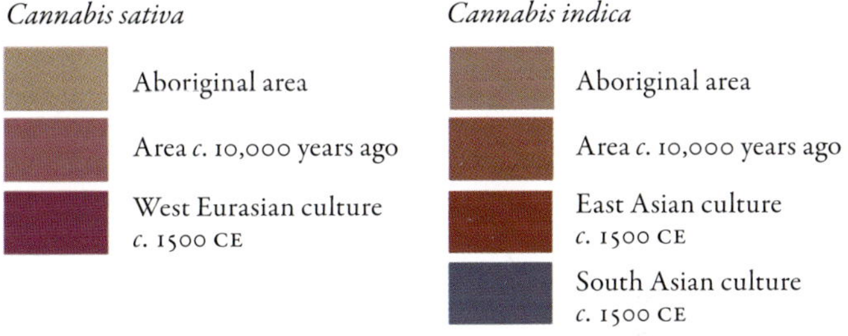

Ancient cannabis zones in Eurasia.

poppyseeds. A translation of an old manuscript called *Pahlavi Texts* by Edward William West in 1901 mentions its use to produce a valuable oil for medicinal purposes, which has a rich history in the region. Renowned medical practitioners such as Rhazes (865–925 CE) and Avicenna (980–1037 CE) ushered in what scholars refer to as the golden age of Persian medicine that lasted into the seventeenth century. An influential manuscript from the period, titled *Bondahesh* (ninth century CE), classified all plants into various categories, with cannabis placed in the group of 'oily herbs' because of the medicinal oil that people extracted from its seed.

Eating these seeds was considered a common form of nutrition in Persia, which became Iran in the 1920s. My father, Mohammad Borougerdi, immigrated to the United States from the country in 1974, before which he used to eat roasted hempseeds as a snack while growing up: 'kind of like eating a bag of chips in the United States today, we sometimes walked around with them in our pockets, taking them out to eat a handful or two whenever we felt like it. They were good to eat.' When he arrived in the United States, however, such snacks were very hard to come by, for cannabis seeds had already become known more as something that people planted clandestinely for countercultural consumption than anything else.

In Europe they have been associated with food rituals and a variety of medicines. A consumable oil derived from them, which was more prevalent among Slavic and eastern European cultures, had become a valuable commodity by the Middle Ages. The anthropologist Vera Rubin's edited volume *Cannabis and Culture* (1975) offers chapters that highlight the rich cultural traditions of ritualistic seed use patterns in the region. The nomadic Scythians are often cited as a cultural group that spread such customs across the continent, where they became integrated into various cultures over time. A hempseed soup called *siemieniotka* is a traditional food in Poland and Lithuania that people still consume, often as part of holiday traditions.

Versions of this dish were integrated into Russian cuisine as well, where hempseed became a staple food for large numbers of serfs living throughout the countryside. They also consumed hempseed oil, which became an important fat and protein source for the Russian population during the nineteenth and twentieth centuries. In addition, several hemp-derived products were important export items that connected Russia to European powers in need of the highest quality fibre for rigging their ships during the Age of Exploration (1400s–1700s). However, after the Bolshevik Revolution (1917) gave way to a devastating civil war that lasted until 1922, Russian hemp exports significantly declined. In 1925 the Soviets still cultivated hemp on roughly 817,000 hectares (2 million ac) of land across the country, but much of those harvests were needed as a food source for domestic consumption.[2]

Russian hempseed oil.

After the Second World War, associations between hemp and marijuana contributed to a significant decline in global consumption. Domestic markets still existed in Italy, France, Romania, Hungary, Turkey, China, Korea, Japan and throughout the Soviet Union, but international prohibitionary measures restricted its production. The rise of synthetic fibres such as rayon and polypropylene also contributed to hemp's demise as an internationally traded commodity. Along the way, some regions of the world with significant cannabis traditions all but lost their culinary connections to the plant. In Georgia, for example, cannabis cuisine went dormant after draconian laws against it were introduced in the twentieth century. The Svan people have a traditional dish of cheesy bread known as *khachapuri* that used to contain cannabis as an ingredient, but a local resident in Tbilisi explained to a journalist how 'it's impossible to find these days – everyone's too afraid of getting caught.'[3]

Hempseed has also belonged to a culture of consumption throughout India that goes back a long time, but a drinkable concoction derived from other plant parts is more common. Today, for example, cannabis seeds and their oil are widely used throughout the country, but bhang is considered a refreshing beverage for more than 30 million people each year. There is a bit of confusion about this word in the English language, however, for in Hindi it can refer to the leaves and stems of cannabis or to the plant more generally, whether psychoactive or otherwise. But bhang also refers to a mildly psychoactive drink that many Hindus consume during festivals such as Holi, which celebrates the arrival of spring. Fragments of cannabis leaves, stems and seeds are pulverized with water into a paste, which then gets mixed with spices and steeped in milk or some other lipid before being strained. The types of spices vary from region to region, but milk is usually part of the recipe because

Unknown artist, *Group of Bhang Addicts*, 1590, gouache on paper.

cannabinoids are not soluble in water. So long as a fat source is used for the molecules to bind to, then a consumer will feel the effects.

Despite the plant's popularity in India, cannabis has continued to have significant legal restrictions on it since the country gained independence in 1947. Exceptions were granted for bhang, but the United Nations (UN) became more stringent against the plant with its Single Convention on Narcotic Drugs (1961). This meant that member states had to criminalize cannabis and declare that it had no medical value, but delegates from India and Iran pushed for the leaves to be omitted from the official language of the convention. They succeeded in getting the UN to agree that 'Cannabis means the flowering or fruiting tops of the cannabis plant (excluding the seeds and leaves when not accompanied by the tops) from which the resin has not been extracted, by whatever name they may be designated.'[4] Since bhang contained parts of the plant that were excluded from the definition, government-sanctioned shops in India were still able to serve the beverage.

The convention's definition certainly established a grey area when it came to psychoactive preparations of the plant, for even though bhang was often described as a mild intoxicant, cannabis leaves have varying degrees of trichomes that grow on their surface. The smaller ones are known as sugar leaves, which protrude out from the ripening female flower clusters. They contain much higher levels of cannabinoids than do the larger fan leaves that grow throughout the life cycle of male and female plants. Sugar leaves often appear frosty as the plant ripens because of the high concentration of trichomes they contain. On the contrary, fan leaves barely contain traces of cannabinoids, so the quantity and quality of plant material used to make bhang matters when gauging its effects.

Historically, the drink has been associated more with the upper classes in India, whereas a preparation known as charas is more connected to the lower segments of the caste system. Along with ganja, or dried buds, charas is usually smoked in a small pipe called a chillum and is more potent because it consists of pure resin collected from the cannabis plant. Although class distinctions based on use existed in India prior to British colonial control, we will see later how the empire played a crucial role in shaping perceptions and codifying categories of cannabis consumption during the nineteenth century.

'Hashish' is a more ubiquitous term than 'charas' that also refers to various preparations of collected cannabis resin, which gets decarboxylated to become psychoactive when smoked. Use of this resin has a long history that originated in Asia and dispersed throughout (and beyond) the continent over the course of centuries. One of the most popular confections derived from it is majoun. There are many different recipes from Morocco, Egypt, India and the Middle East, but most consist of hashish mixed with some variation of nuts, dried fruit, fudge and honey, combined with various spices. During the nineteenth century, it became popular among subcultures in the Atlantic world that developed an attachment to the exoticized concept of the Orient. As a set of cultural representations of the East that both attracted and repulsed Western minds, Orientalism inspired some Europeans and U.S. Americans to embrace the concept

Microscopic close-up of a cannabis sugar leaf.

Modern majoun.

that one scholar referred to as 'playing Eastern'.[5] Majoun became part of the discourse.

One example comes from Paris in the 1840s, when psychoactive cannabis had just become integrated with Western medicine. At the time, medical practitioners often described the plant as both a blessing and a curse. References to its use as a noxious drug in the East usually appeared in medical descriptions that included warnings of the plant's potential dangers, but they also touted its value as a healing agent for several ailments. A few French medical practitioners contributed to these discussions before the Club des Hashischins emerged, which met for monthly meetings at a Parisian hotel between 1844 and 1849. At these meetings, Jacques-Joseph Moreau de Tours played Eastern by dressing up in orientalized costume while he served an edible cannabis paste to the guests, who often included literary figures such as Charles Baudelaire, Victor Hugo and Alexandre Dumas.

The edible concoction served at these dinners was majoun. It's often referred to as hashish, but again, that's a term more accurately used to describe several different concentrated forms of cannabis resin. Majoun, on the other hand, refers to an edible confection made with cannabis resin as an ingredient. Some also called it dawamesk, which nineteenth-century sources in the United States repackaged as 'Hasheesh candy'. Advertisements with exotic, orientalized descriptions of these sweets appeared in a few sources across the country, until the plant's criminalization caused different consumption patterns to develop among new cannabis users.[6]

Cultivation and Production

Cannabis is quite an adaptable plant that grows feral in many regions around the world. It likes well-draining, fertile soil and can survive in temperatures ranging from 10°C to more than 38°C. Different varieties reach from around 1 to 5 metres (3–16 ft) tall when they are fully grown. Some types are shorter and bushier, while others take up significant surface area and branch out like trees. When cultivated for hemp fibre, they are sown so densely together that weeds do not become invasive underneath the canopy of green growth, whereas plants grown for buds are given more space to develop denser flowers.

Slightly more acidic soils help cannabis to absorb nutrients through its intricate root system, which in addition to nitrogen also requires lots of phosphorous and potassium (N-P-K) over the course of the plant's life cycle. Quite a few trace minerals are important for high-quality bud production as well, which start to grow on the females once they are limited to twelve hours of sunlight each day. Both male and female flowers can grow on the same plant in some genetic combinations, or if they are exposed to various amounts of stress, but none of this usually begins until light exposure decreases. Plants that exhibit this type of photoperiodism are called long-day plants (LDPs), but some cannabis cultivars will transition into the flowering stage automatically without needing twelve hours of darkness. These have become known as auto-flowering varieties.

Before the mid-nineteenth century, Western nations cultivated cannabis mostly for its fibre. The quality of harvests varied significantly from region to region across time and space, but Russia has historically been known for producing the best crops. Most associated it with compulsory types of labour regimes, such as Russian serfdom, peasants in Europe

African American man processing hemp stalks for fibre at a farm in Lexington, Kentucky, n.d.

Beating hemp in Bridewell prison: William Hogarth, *A Harlot's Progress Plate IV*, 1732, engraving.

and enslaved Africans or sharecropping African Americans in the United States. Criminals were also forced to process the fibre. An eighteenth-century British source included 'strumpets', which refers to female prostitutes, in the category of those 'who were made to beat hemp'.[7] These associations between processing cannabis fibre, criminality and tedious work are important pieces in the puzzle of why the plant fell out of favour during the twentieth century.

Another piece revolves around perceptions of drug cannabis as some sort of sinister Asiatic intoxicant, which seems to have overshadowed its use as a medicine in the West almost as soon as it was introduced during the 1830s. Most of the plant parts Europeans and Americans used for this were imported from India, where the British developed a civilizing mission that eventually brought them in contact with cannabis cultivation techniques they had never seen before. In the 1870s the

Preparing flat ganja, Naogaon, Bangladesh, 1894.

colonial government commissioned a deputy collector named Hem Chunder Kerr to research its cultivation, production and distribution in British India, for which he visited 'ganja villages', cultivation centres that made some of the highest-quality cannabis buds in the world at the time.

The report came out in 1876 and listed several valuable regions, with Bengal considered the most celebrated. Kerr claimed the 'ganja cultivators' there produced more than 60,000 maunds of ganja per year by the early nineteenth century, which is roughly 2.2 million kilograms (4.8 million lb).[8] He referred to the largest centre in the region as the 'Ganja Mahal', where a 24,280 hectare (60,000 ac) tract of land produced various grades of cannabis on a rotating basis with several other crops. The cultivators had to plough the soil several times over a period of months before planting, with multiple rounds of composting and quality soil infusions between each plough.

Nutrient-rich rows of raised mounds several inches high served as the site to grow transplants that were carefully selected from a nearby nursery.

After a few weeks of transitioning into the flowering stage, cultivators had to call in a craftsman whom Kerr referred to as a 'ganja doctor'. These specialists inspected the rows for signs of male flowers, which meant those plants needed to be removed before they had a chance to pollinate the females. When female cannabis plants are deprived of male pollen, their pistillate flowers swell up into dense clusters along the sides of the stems and branches. These unpollinated buds are often called *sinsemilla* (Spanish for 'without seeds') or 'sensi' flowers today. They are the most potent part of the plant, which the ganja doctor protected by inspecting each one carefully for male flowers over the next four weeks. If done well, a crop of fully matured, seedless female cannabis plants would be harvested after several months of growth at the Ganja Mahal.

Nearly two decades after Kerr's report, British parliament appointed the Indian Hemp Drugs Commission (IHDC) to expand on his findings. The committee for the IHDC published its report in 1894, which included thousands of pages on the use, cultivation, production and history of cannabis drugs across various regions of British India. The report is a significant source for several reasons, but how it expanded upon Kerr's insight into growing seedless female plants led to improvements in the cultivation process that eventually transformed cannabis buds into higher-quality, medical-grade products of immense value. It wasn't until the seismic shift towards indoor gardening took place a century later that these improvements revolutionized the cannabis industry, however. In the meantime, perceptions of the plant as a noxious Asiatic intoxicant disrupted its place in Western societies, resulting in a culture war that criminalized its cultivation and production.

As a result, today, a significant amount of cannabis is grown illegally behind closed doors. It is hard to determine exactly how much, but thousands of people show up to conventions in cities across Europe and the Americas every year to buy seeds from breeders so that they can plant them in places where it's against the law. Cultivators have developed transatlantic networks of knowledge exchange on how best to avoid detection, where to set up grow operations for maximum productivity and how to ensure the highest-quality harvests. At great risk to their personal freedom, thousands of people invest significant time and energy into a rather complicated process that could be raided at any moment. Some of them do it for money, but others do it out of devotion for the plant. 'Guerrilla warfare' is a term often used to describe how an outmatched opponent operates against a more formidable foe during times of war, but it is an apt expression for these clandestine indoor operations as well. One might even call them 'guerrilla gardens', which have been on the rise since the 1980s.[9]

Before then, few cannabis consumers in Europe or the United States knew much about the value of separating male and female plants to improve potency. Word of the IHDC's report started circulating across the Atlantic shortly after its publication, but it's hard to gauge how many people read it or came across its references to the cultivation technique for producing *sinsemilla* bud. An article from *Physicians Drug News* in 1915 described how 'fertilization interferes with yield of resin', which is why the author described how the 'male flowers are removed'.[10] There are others as well, but prior to the twentieth century, most drug cannabis in Western countries came from India via the British empire. The trend had shifted slightly by the 1920s, with references to removing male plants increasing in the decades that followed.[11] Cannabis cultivation had also increased in Mexico by then, where the plant's reputation

Flowering cannabis growing indoors, unknown location, 2016.

diminished significantly as it became more connected with the word 'marihuana'.

The trend towards suspicion and criminalization belonged to a larger context that included a global anti-drug crusade adopted by the League of Nations, which focused more on the plant as a social problem in the 1930s. The international momentum against certain cultural consumption patterns of drug use had been on the rise since the second half of the nineteenth century, with cannabis becoming the next target. Mexican migrant workers and African American jazz musicians in the United States, as well as Hindus, Muslims and Afro-Caribbeans from cannabis-consuming societies within the British empire, became heavily associated with different variations of the drug during this period. The repulsive aspects of Orientalism intensified these associations, leading to a draconian system of international control that had criminalized cannabis cultivation, distribution and consumption by the 1950s.

When the trend towards global prohibition broke out, cannabis cultivation took place primarily outdoors. But increased penalties for smuggling and more frequent raids on production sites caused growers to adapt ways to apply the techniques Kerr described at the Ganja Mahal to a more controlled environment, under artificial lighting, with an ever-expanding array of technological innovations for optimizing the quality of cannabis they grew. The industry of hydroponics, a technique that involves growing plants in containers with a soilless medium such as rocks or gravel and submerging them in a nutrient solution, became a key factor in this transition as well. The idea has been around for centuries, but as an industry, it didn't garner much interest until the second half of the twentieth century – just as cannabis cultivators were searching for new ways to improve their clandestine operations.

By the 1970s ads were appearing in countercultural magazines such as *High Times* that offered home-cultivation kits for

Workers for the New York City Department of Sanitation removing growth of cannabis plants, 1958.

'Pot Patriots' who wanted to produce their own crops. The first edition that referenced hydroponics appeared in 1976, shortly after the United States and Mexico established what they called 'Operation Clearview'. Essentially the U.S. government provided Mexico with funds to conduct flight missions over suspected cultivation sites and spray a chemical known as Paraquat to poison the vegetation. *High Times* responded by publishing articles that condemned the initiative, decrying how this 'terror in the fields' caused 'tension to the line of supply'. With hydroponics, clandestine cultivators could transform their 'closets and attics' into their 'own secret Eden', free from the worries of contaminated crops and supply shortages.[12]

As the hydroponic industry became more sophisticated, *High Times* increased the space and frequency of its ads. More equipment for growers to choose from appeared alongside an assortment of nutrient solutions containing guidelines on how to use them for each stage of the plant's life cycle. Devices to disperse CO_2 within confined spaces increased crop yields, and lighting systems provided spectrums that mimicked the sun. Trellises were developed to hold up the increasingly heavy branches of engorged buds that were soaking up chemical cocktails through their root systems. Circulation pumps transported these chemicals from reservoirs containing precise formula solutions that needed to be mixed and replaced each week. Testing gauges helped cultivators determine water quality, measure pH and check the parts per million of chemicals in the water to maximize plant intakes. The transformation was quite profound.

Demand increased so much that, by the 2010s, 1 kilogram (2 lb) of the highest-quality harvest could cost more than £6,400 ($10,000). Ed Rosenthal was a prominent cultivator on the international scene during this transition. In 1978 he and Mel Frank published the *Marijuana Grower's Guide*, which has

High-quality cannabis bud.

gone through several editions and sold more than a million copies over the decades. Guerrilla gardening in California during the 1970s with seeds collected from around the world, Frank and Rosenthal experimented with cross-breeding cannabis to create new hybrids. They also established techniques for propagating clones from mother plants, which removed the need for ganja doctors to invest so much time and energy inspecting the grow site for male plants. When cultivators started leaving the United States for the more tolerant culture that developed in Spain after the fall of Franco's dictatorship, they took Frank and Rosenthal's seeds with them. These cultivars made their way into the Netherlands, too, which emerged as one of the world's largest and most vibrant epicentres of cannabis culture.

In fact *High Times* held its first Cannabis Cup festival in Amsterdam, which took place in 1988. Like in Spain, cannabis was (and still is) technically illegal in the Netherlands, but possession of small amounts and cultivation of a few plants is tolerated. No legal right has ever existed for cannabis coffee shops to purchase the products they sell, but the Dutch term *gedoogbeleid* reflects the policy of tolerance that allows transactions to take place discreetly. There is also a limit to how much cannabis the shops can possess, and they can only sell small amounts to their customers. Although complicated, the system has spurred a transnational culture of connoisseurship for those who value high-quality cannabis. The festival spread to other cities as well by the 1990s, as did the variety of products people submitted to the competition. The connoisseur culture became so immense that one breeder from California, who goes by the name Capulator, sold a package of ten seeds from one of his crops at an auction for £13,800 ($17,000) in 2016. He called it MAC, which is short for 'Miracle Alien Cookies'.[13]

Clearly, cannabis has transformed drastically since the days of the Ganja Mahal, just not in the way that prohibitionists had envisioned. Improvements to the quality, taste and flavour of

Cannabis products at a coffee shop in Amsterdam, 2022.

the plant have paved the way for a multi-billion-pound medical and recreational industry that has made the idea of eating and drinking it more appealing than ever. But what, exactly, makes cannabis consumption so attractive to people in the first place?

2
Cannabis Chemistry and Pharmacology

Hand in hand with cannabis's use as a medicine
went its abuse as an intoxicant.
Ernest L. Abel, *A Comprehensive Guide to the Cannabis Literature* (1979)

Although people have consumed cannabis for thousands of years, modern scientific understanding of its effects is limited and relatively new. For one, laboratory chemists didn't identify the plant's primary psychoactive compound until more than a century after they isolated morphine from opium (1804) and cocaine from the coca shrub (1859). The complexity of cannabis chemistry made it difficult for these researchers to identify its compounds with the methods and techniques used to isolate alkaloids, so consumers and medical practitioners were left with speculations and flawed experiments to guide their assumptions.

Finally, however, in 1964, after the plant had begun its transition into a global symbol of transgressive countercultural identity, an organic chemist at the Hebrew University of Jerusalem named Raphael Mechoulam isolated THC and elucidated its structure. This sparked a wave of research that, by the 1990s, had led him and others to discover the human body's endocannabinoid system (ECS). It's like a cell-signalling network within our nervous system that contains its own naturally occurring cannabinoids and cannabinoid receptors. The ECS is responsible for regulating a variety of bodily responses, including mood, appetite, pain perception, coordination and a range of cognitive and immune system functions. The rise of a transnational drug control culture has severely limited the nature of this research on a global scale, but it hasn't stopped scientists from learning more about the plant's therapeutic potential.

It has, however, unleashed a complex discourse that obfuscates the narrative, making it hard to 'see through the smoke', as one physician alluded to in the title of his 2023 book on the subject.[1] An entangled web of legal, cultural and medical perspectives has woven into a Gordian knot of erroneous assertions and misconceptions, blurring the line between fact and fiction when it comes to understanding how cannabis affects the mind. Thomas Kuhn's seminal work *The Structure of Scientific Revolutions* (1962) emphasized the pivotal role that subjectivity

THC's molecular structure.

can play in shaping the character of scientific knowledge, which proved to be particularly significant for cannabis. His theory helps explain how, as Western societies gained more exposure to the plant's different uses, preconceived notions of Oriental depravity were ingrained in its meaning, thereby shaping the nature of their scientific research.

In the United States, for example, perceptions of drug use have been so infused with conceptions of vice and degeneracy that many people simply cannot fathom the idea of cannabis consumption as part of a healthy, responsible lifestyle. In his 2021 book *Drug Use for Grown-Ups*, the neuroscientist Carl Hart explains how these societal perceptions influence the scientific process by predisposing scientists to begin their research with cultural assumptions and preconceived notions that drive them to overstate the evidence and distort the results. Media outlets exacerbate the problem by cherry-picking catchphrases from the abstracts of scientific publications without ever really investigating the data used in the study.

These snippets of information then get reduced to sensationalized headlines that politicians often transform into policy through racism or fearmongering. The publicly sanctioned ignorance gets passed off as knowledge and accepted as truth, which justifies the need for more social control over genuine understanding. This could explain why research from the 1930s into cannabis's potential for alleviating symptoms of epilepsy were minimized or ignored because it didn't fit into the narrative of 'Reefer Madness' that dominated the discourse back then. Today, although it still takes some time and effort to sift through the negative sensationalism about the plant, there is a lot more evidence to support the concept that cannabis is, in fact, more of a medicine than the soul-sapping substance of death that drug war crusaders have tried to make it out to be over the past century or so.

'If you want a good smoke, try one of these': *Reefer Madness* (1936, dir. Louis J. Gasnier), described as a cautionary tale on the use of marijuana.

This is not to suggest that there aren't any concerns when it comes to cannabis consumption, however, especially within specific sociocultural contexts. For example, research has found a correlation between increased cannabis use and the prevalence of certain psychiatric illnesses such as depression, anxiety, insomnia and schizophrenia. These risk factors seem to increase when consumption begins before the age of eighteen or if the user is predisposed to certain mental health conditions. Moreover, the latest version of the *Diagnostic and Statistical Manual of Mental Disorders* – or DSM-5-TR – defines Cannabis Use Disorder (CUD) as a form of compulsive consumption where the user can't quit despite experiencing negative consequences connected to their use. Some statistics even suggest that as many as 10 per cent of heavy users develop this disorder, the symptoms of which include adverse effects on personal or family relationships, a decline in school performance or extracurricular activities or the inability to fulfil one's work obligations due to compulsively consuming cannabis.

The findings warrant careful consideration, but it's also important to acknowledge that correlation does not imply causation. Yet journalists and their news agencies consistently present the research with unwavering conviction, treating it as indisputable truth. This hasty acceptance often stems from the tendency to blame drugs for deeper, more systemic issues. Socioeconomic and psychological conditions such as poverty, social marginalization, trauma, stress and co-occurring psychiatric illnesses, for instance, are all factors that correlate to the development of substance use disorders. However, major institutions such as the National Institute of Drug Abuse (NIDA) in the United States frame all non-medical drug use through the lens of dysfunctional behaviour, deeming it problematic by nature and always ill-advised. This framing diverts societal attention from the root causes of addiction and perpetuates the very problem that the institution claims it wants to fix.

Such a framework has dominated the discourse around cannabis throughout the twentieth century, but the pendulum seems to be swinging away from it now, with more scientific research focusing on the therapeutic potential of the plant's chemical compounds.

Terpenes, Flavonoids and Cannabinoids

The pungent smell that emanates from cannabis varies widely but becomes stronger as the plant's flower clusters develop – especially in the females. Their buds contain microscopic glands known as trichomes that are packed with different genetic combinations of chemical compounds. Each cannabis plant grown from seed has its own unique chemical profile that contains

Cannabis trichomes growing on a sugar leaf.

large concentrations of these chemicals. One of them is a diverse class of aromatic compounds called terpenes. Along with a range of purported therapeutic properties, they are what give cannabis its citrusy, floral, fruity, piney, peppery, lavender- or lilac-like smells and flavours. Research also suggests they work in tandem with the plant's other compounds to improve its medical potential or enhance its psychoactive effects. Cannabis specialists call this 'the entourage effect', which Peter Grinspoon describes as 'the effectiveness of the main therapeutic (and intoxicating) molecule THC [being] enhanced by the synergistic effects of the different cannabinoids and, likely, terpenes and flavonoids working together'.[2]

Although not as prevalent as terpenes, flavonoids are also important. They have an impact on the plant's colouration and exhibit a variety of therapeutic properties as well. Cannabis that contains high concentrations of a terpene called caryophyllene and the flavonoid anthocyanin, for example, might exhibit hues of purple or lavender with an olfactory reminiscent of pepper or cloves, whereas another variety with the terpene limonene and a flavone called apigenin would smell like citrus and look more yellow. Both would also contain anti-inflammatory and antioxidant properties. Research comparing the therapeutic potential between cannabis plants with different genetic combinations of these compounds is still quite nascent, but colloquial descriptions of the effect that some of the more common strains have on consumers do exist in dispensaries and underground markets. They're not always consistent, however.

For instance, the effects of a strain called Girl Scout Cookies (GSC) at a dispensary in Colorado might be strikingly different from the same strain at a dispensary in California. If both cultivators had grown their batches of GSC from a stabilized seed source, then theoretically they could turn out similar. However, the plant's chemical profile can vary widely based on the environmental conditions under which it is grown – as well as the method of cultivation used to grow it. Not only that but even stabilized seed stocks of cannabis can exhibit genetic variation, depending on the breeding practices and seed-selection process of the breeder who produced the hybrid. Genetic variation even occurs in landrace cultivars, in fact, which refers to indigenous varieties that have developed naturally within a native region over a long time (think heirloom, for example). All of

Indoor operation in the United States where a cannabis cultivar is being grown using the 'Sea of Green' method, 2023.

this makes it very difficult to standardize the cannabis industry, which is filled with strains that carry the same name but deliver different experiences.

Of course, none of these plants would be as appealing to those who consume them without the cannabinoids that are also found in the trichomes. Scientists have identified more than one hundred of them, with tetrahydrocannabinol (THC) considered the most psychoactive. Cannabidiol (CBD) is the most popular non-psychoactive one today. Recently relegalized variations of cannabis (hemp) contain higher percentages of CBD without testing positive for too much THC. Consequently, they offer a legal means for consumers to explore some of the plant's therapeutic potential without experiencing its psychoactive effects. The CBD market has faced tremendous challenges, but it has still become a multi-billion-pound industry. Although scientific knowledge of its effects is evolving, studies have shown its potential for treating some forms of epilepsy, anxiety and chronic pain. There's not much conclusive evidence on the efficacy of all those CBD-infused products that keep flooding into international markets, however.

In fact, of all the other cannabinoids that chemists have identified within the plant thus far, only a handful have been the subjects of scientific studies. These include cannabigerol (CBG), cannabinol (CBN) and cannabichromene (CBC). CBG studies suggest it is a neuroprotective agent that is also an anti-inflammatory, while research into CBN shows signs of its sedative effects. CBC could be a valuable antifungal and antibacterial agent that can also relieve pain and improve mood, but again, the evidence isn't concrete and still requires more work with clinical trials before it can be confirmed with confidence. What does seem clear from the evidence, however, is that investing in this approach has far more social utility than waging a war against the plant.[3]

CBD store in France, 2022.

We also know that it's not just the cannabinoid profile of a cannabis strain that contributes to its nuanced psychoactive effects. However, the complexity behind this 'entourage effect' gets reduced to generalized assumptions about so-called indica and sativa varieties at dispensaries. Categorizing psychoactive cannabis by this dichotomy is confusing because these terms have historically been used to distinguish non-psychoactive species (sativa) from psychoactive ones (indica). From the more taxonomically historical, species-oriented perspective of these terms, for example, what the colloquial cannabis cultures call sativa and indica are actually references to different cultivars of *Cannabis indica*. The ones they call sativa are really indica variations that grow taller, have a narrower leaf structure and contain a chemical profile that is known for its uplifting or energetic psychoactive effects. However, strains that dispensaries call indica are psychoactive cultivars that grow short and bushy, have a broader leaf structure and deliver a more relaxing or sedative high.

Clearly, cannabis nomenclature needs a serious overhaul, which is likely to occur as the industry evolves and marketing teams learn more about the various combinations of chemical compounds it produces. Terpene, flavonoid and cannabinoid profiles are more accurate indicators of the plant's physiological effects on its consumers, but even they don't paint the whole picture. How long the trichomes that house these chemicals have been allowed to ripen before they are harvested also contributes to the pharmacological effects they have on the human mind. Not only that, but the psychological state of the one who consumes the drug, as well as the cultural setting in which consumption occurs, are both vital factors in shaping the nature of a cannabis experience.

The Psychoactive Riddle

The symbiotic connection between these three elements of cannabis consumption – the pharmacology, the mind and the culture – is difficult to unpack. The historian Isaac Campos calls it a 'psychoactive riddle' because there's 'a complex tangle' between them that shapes the effects the drug has on the body and mind of its user.[4] To unravel this entanglement, one must consider the history of an individual's consumption, as well as the society and culture in which the consumption pattern formed. However, the cult of pharmacology has prevented such considerations by denying they even exist. Richard DeGrandpre coined this term to denote the belief that drugs have special powers that make them 'capable of bypassing all the social conditioning of the mind, directly transforming the drug user's thoughts and action' in a set and predetermined way. The cult developed alongside modern science by replacing people's faith in magic with the belief in a pharmacological essence 'contained within the drug's chemical structure [that] determine[s] drug outcomes in the body, the brain, and behaviour'.[5]

The so-called war on drugs reflects this way of thinking because it reduces them to black-and-white categories of good and evil substances that need to be contained and controlled. Oftentimes, however, cultures construct these moral distinctions based on aspects of the drug that have little to do with chemistry, such as the way Orientalism helped cannabis develop a reputation for inducing violence and insanity before the plant became part of Western medicine. Eastern stories from *The Thousand and One Nights* offered some suggestions about cannabis-induced states, which evolved into idiomatic references to users in the subcontinent of Southeast Asia by the early nineteenth century. Stereotypes of degenerate 'half savages' perpetuated by travel writers such as Richard F. Burton, for example, popularized the perception that 'running amok' was a 'hysterical affection of certain races inhabiting oriental countries', which many attributed to their use of 'the extract of hemp called bhang, ganja, or charras'.[6]

These perceptions were widespread and consistent across time and space. Campos's research into them coming out of Mexico reveals 'there was almost no counter discourse' to the 'madness' narrative, while the British reported extensively on the idea that cannabis consumption was the reason why so many patients were admitted to 'the lunatic asylums of India'.[7] Similar observations coming out of France and the United States were

Exoticized illustration by John D. Batten, from E. Dixon, ed., *Fairy Tales from the Arabian Nights* (1915?).

pervasive as well, which together reflect what DeGrandpre dubbed 'a placebo text' to describe 'the cultural teachings that inform the beliefs and expectations about a drug'.[8] These expectations evoke a response the same way a placebo can affect the outcome of an experience someone has who thinks they've consumed a drug. Like a cultural placebo of sorts.

To be sure, cannabis does have hallucinogenic properties, even if they are much milder than those that are officially classified as psychedelics. Adverse effects from overdosing usually consists of high anxiety and increased paranoia, especially if consumption takes place under unexpected circumstances or in unfamiliar settings among novice users. Tolerance is a protective mechanism that can develop over time to help guard against this reaction, but it can still occur among experienced cannabis consumers. Until recently, researchers did not have the capacity to understand how dosage affects these adverse reactions, so the Orientalist-infused placebo text informed their explanations.

Route of administration is also a crucial consideration in cannabis pharmacology: the effects take much longer to manifest when ingested compared to smoking. Titration, or the process of adjusting the dosage for a desired effect, becomes less predictable due to individualized variations such as metabolism, tolerance and the unique response each person has to cannabinoids. Other factors such as fat levels in the bloodstream and recent dietary intake influence the outcome of eating it as well. Since most cannabis used in Western medicine during the nineteenth and early twentieth centuries was administered orally, people likely had a difficult time gauging how much of it to consume – which explains the effects that literary figures such as Fitz Hugh Ludlow, Bayard Taylor and members of the Club des Hashischins described in their vivid depictions of cannabis-induced hallucinations.

Of course, the fact that these medical preparations were concocted with limited knowledge of the plant's psychoactive properties and often contained ingredients that are no longer considered safe for medical use further complicated the matter. There is a lot more information available now than there was a century ago, but there is still so much research that needs to be done. Over 32,000 scientific studies have been conducted in the past decade, for example, but still only a handful of cannabinoids have been put to the test.[9] Before deciding whether cannabis is the right solution to any of the problems it can potentially alleviate, it is advisable to learn as much as possible about the plant and to seek guidance from an experienced medical professional.

But for now, it's time to get back to a part of the plant that has almost nothing to do with its drug components yet has still played a major part in world history.

3
Hempseed in World History

Let them eat hemp.
Sydney Morning Herald (2014)

For a long time, hempseed has been a part of the theatrical drama we might call world history. It makes an appearance across the globe at different stages on various levels of prominence throughout the play. Efforts to prohibit its production skyrocketed in the twentieth century, when fears of cannabis drugs reached such heights that governments started attacking the entire plant. By the 1980s, however – just as the shift towards indoor hydroponic gardening was taking off – hemp activists brought it back onto the global stage as a legitimate commodity. Today, one might say we are in a renaissance of sorts for hempseed consumption, with cookbooks and consumable products popping up all over the place designed to convince people of the value of eating this highly nutritious food.

One of the earliest significant associations with hempseed consumption in world history goes back to the legend of Siddhartha Gautama, which sources have referenced since at least the third century CE. Even today, it inspires hemp enthusiasts such as Fabian Braitsch in Austria, who founded a hemp food company called Hempions. He advocates eating hemp products as part of a balanced diet, but he also wrote about an experiment he conducted in 2018 by eating nothing but hempseed for 22 consecutive days, which he called the 'Buddha Diet'. As the title suggests, the Buddhist legend 'was the reason for our founder Fabian to eat only hemp seeds for weeks'.[1] It didn't seem like an enjoyable experience, but he made it through, losing 7 kilograms (15 lb) of weight in the process.

Fabian's example reflects how persistent the connection between hemp and health has been since Buddha's time, which has endured despite the onslaught of a global drug war against the plant. Today, many types of innovative food preparations contain hempseed as an ingredient. There's hempseed soup, cereal, granola and smoothies of all sorts, for example,

Fabian Braitsch of Hempions with his healthy hemp food products.

Hempseed carrot cake at a café in Finland, 2020.

Breakfast cookies with hemp hearts.

as well as hempseed carrot cake, hempseed pesto and hempseed tabbouleh. Hempseed ranch houmous, turmeric hempseed protein bars and sweet potato hempseed quinoa bowls also exist. People sprinkle crushed hempseed onto their salads and make healthy breakfast cookies out of their crushed insides – known as hemp hearts. There is even a creamy cauliflower hempseed alfredo sauce that people can pour onto a dish of veggie nuggets with broccoli, hempseed and millet.

Yet this highly nutritious seed didn't always have the versatile reputation it has today.

Old World to New World

Despite the popularity of hempseed foods that emerged during the last two decades of the twentieth century, consuming it has historically not been very fashionable. In fact, for most of recorded history, those who consumed it did so reluctantly. It does seem to have been common in China during the Zhou dynasty (1046–256 BCE), but cannabis use for medicinal and fibrous purposes surpassed it as a food source in the centuries after the Han dynasty (202 BCE–220 CE) consolidated power. It became a staple crop for a while during the Tang dynasty (618–906 CE), but not for long. Ancient Sanskrit sources from South Asia also referenced hempseed as a food source, but people there considered the plant to be more of a medicine than anything else. Elaborate trade networks stitched vast regions together on what became known as the Silk Road, along which cannabis was dispersed over the course of centuries.

At some point, it reached beyond these routes into South and East Africa. African societies used cannabis for multiple purposes as well, but its primary function was as a smokeable drug. The earliest evidence points to Madagascar as the first region it landed before crossing the continent. Some regions also cultivated it as a fibre, with Madagascar and later Mozambique having done so on a large scale. Male pollen dating from 1800 BCE has been analysed by archaeologists who discovered it in Botswana, but they don't know how it got there. Racial stereotypes and Eurocentric interpretations of history have minimized African contributions to plant knowledge, which for cannabis has been vital.[2]

The plant arrived in North Africa via the Mediterranean, with male pollen having been discovered in Egypt as far back as 2500 BCE. But again, it is difficult to pinpoint how it got there. The Maghreb region of North Africa, however, showed signs of cannabis cultures with increasing prevalence between 300 and 1000 CE, when it became abundant in Morocco. Over centuries, the plant was woven into the rich culture of smoking there as well, for which Africans developed sophisticated pipe technologies that eventually influenced smoking cultures around the world. Evidence of eating cannabis seeds, however, does not show up as a prevalent cultural custom anywhere on the continent until much later in the historical record. For some reason, they were just not that appealing.

In Europe there is far less biodiversity across the continent than in Africa, which could explain why hempseed has a much longer historical association as a food there – albeit a reluctant one. Lots of evidence reveals the plant's use as a fibre and a non-psychoactive medicinal oil or seed, but it's hard to tell from the available sources how often Europeans ate it prior to the twentieth century – beyond a few traditions from eastern Europe, Poland, Russia, Eurasia and the Caucasus. When it did get mentioned as a food source, it often occurred under dire circumstances. An eighteenth-century medical text, for example, details an entry about hempseed: 'in times of Distress Men have attempted to live upon it; but it has not succeeded well, occasioning violent and continued Disorders of the Head'.[3]

Instead, hempseed played a more prominent part in household medicines. As one manuscript noted, the ingredient was 'so well known to every good Housewife in the Country, that I shall not need to write any Description of it', before delving into how it can be 'boiled in Milk and taken [to] helpeth such as have a hot dry cough'. The author claimed that the 'Dutch make an Emulsion out of the Seed and give it with good success to those that have the Jaundice', among other ailments.[4] Eighteenth-century sources often repeated the idea that hempseed needed no introduction owing to its prevalence, with publications on a range of subjects even reflecting its use as a unit of measure. For instance a fishing manual described the need to use an angler that was the 'shape and size of a hemp-seed', while a medical text described a tumour as being 'of the Bigness of a Hemp-seed'. These references were not isolated or limited to eighteenth-century Europe, either, for a medical source from 1901 published in the United States described 'an eruption on the neck' of a patient as being 'the size of a hempseed'.[5]

Its most popular use in Europe prior to the hemp health movement that emerged during the twentieth century, however, was as a source of food for birds and livestock. At least since the early 1700s publications have mentioned the value of feeding it to animals. Hens apparently 'lay more Eggs than with any other sort of Grain' when fed 'Hemp-seed', and it also 'nourishes and warms your Sick *Canary Birds*'.[6] Four ounces of 'boiled hemp seed' given to cows 'will greatly increase the quantity of milk' they produced, while those interested in joining the 'BIRD-FANCIER'S Club' in London could read about its value for attracting songbirds to their homes.[7] Bird feed companies across the United States sold hempseed for such purposes as well, and this practice continued well into the twentieth century.

Before the torrent of transatlantic exchanges erupted between the so-called old and new worlds after 1492, however, cannabis didn't exist in the Americas. Europeans brought it across the Atlantic as a fibre, oil, food ingredient and source of animal feed, while enslaved Africans likely carried it across the ocean for drug purposes. The transatlantic slave trade (1500s–1800s) displaced millions of people through the treacherous journey known as the Middle Passage, and cannabis seeds were small enough to conceal along the way. THC is known for its potential to alleviate some of the pain associated

Cover of the *Birds, Fancy Fish and Sea Shells* catalogue issued by the Iowa Seed Company, 1901.

with enslavement and gruelling labour regimes, which at least 12.5 million Africans experienced by the mid-nineteenth century. In fact, the only historical account that has survived of any European documenting an enslaved African preserving the seeds of a plant comes from a French American traveller named Paul Du Chaillu, who described a captive man off the coast of Gabon saving cannabis seeds, 'carefully preserving them, intending to plant them in the country to which he should be sold'.[8]

Southeast Asians also brought cannabis with them to the Caribbean during the nineteenth century for similar purposes, highlighting the stark contrast between the two distinct pathways by which it came to the Americas, and for what purposes. The European pathway came to represent the legitimate, proper use for the plant, whereas African and Asian associations got labelled as deviant, primitive and sinister. Although little research exists on the history of cannabis use in Native American societies, evidence does suggest that some Indigenous medical practitioners had adopted the plant under the name *pipiltzintzintlis* by the mid-eighteenth century. A Spanish colonizer in New Spain named José Antonio Alzate y Ramírez documented his experience growing seeds he acquired from local *herbolarias* in Mexico that turned out to be cannabis, which they had also called *pipiltzintzintlis*.[9] Spanish perceptions of Indigenous medico-religious plant practices were notoriously harsh, so these uses were labelled as deviant and sinister as well.

Since there are no reproductive barriers between species, different varieties of *Cannabis sativa* and *indica* likely cross-pollinated each other in the Americas over the centuries of exchange, creating hybrid strains with THC/CBD variations at a time before anyone understood cannabis chemistry. The wide-ranging distance that male pollen can travel suggests this cross-pollination was prevalent throughout the dispersal process across the Western hemisphere. European colonists continued to recognize their 'respectable' varieties as they carved the land up into spheres of influence for their respective empires, which

Hempseed growing in a female cannabis flower.

magnified the racialized dichotomy between the different uses. Publications stressing the need to cultivate more cannabis for 'productive' purposes were quite prevalent on both sides of the Atlantic by the end of the eighteenth century, but that all changed significantly over the next hundred years.[10]

Collateral Damage

By the time the First World War (1914–18) came to an end, cannabis was becoming less associated with industry and more representative of something governments saw as a threat. Industrial cannabis cultivation still existed, but references to sinister Asiatic-, Mexican- and African-derived consumption practices threatened to overshadow them. Not only that, but autobiographical drug writing as a literary genre produced by figures such as Samuel Taylor Coleridge, Thomas De Quincey, Bayard Taylor, Fitz Hugh Ludlow, Aleister Crowley and Aldous Huxley (among others) intensified transatlantic perceptions of these 'otherized' uses by infusing them with more exotic descriptions of the plant's mind-altering effects. Medicines made from it were also widely erratic, since chemists and medical practitioners still didn't understand the way cannabinoids functioned, which only exacerbated the problem.

All of this compounded at a time when drug control was being constructed as a major international issue, with multinational organizations such as the League of Nations tapping into the growing transnational movement towards regulation, restriction and social control that had been brewing for decades. International discussions between imperial powers on policing drug cultures had been around at least since the aftermath of the Opium Wars of the mid-nineteenth century, which the League of Nations built upon with its Advisory

Committee on the Traffic in Opium and Other Dangerous Drugs (1920). In 1946 the organization that replaced the League of Nations – the UN – continued this legacy with its Single Convention on Narcotic Drugs (1961).

Granted, cannabis still functioned as a multi-purpose plant within the global economy, but more of its parts were coming under scrutiny due to the growing suspicion behind its use as a drug. In 1935, for example, a report surfaced in the UK about someone who picked some cannabis seeds out of his parrot food to plant in his garden, which he harvested and consumed with his fiancée. Someone alerted the authorities, and word of the incident made it back to a drug enforcement agent who used the opportunity to warn the citizens of Liverpool that it was 'an offence for any person (unless he is licensed or otherwise authorized to do so) to be in possession of, or attempt to obtain possession of, Indian hemp'. Records indicate that such possession in the UK was not very common at the time, but when it was reported, there was an association of foreignness connected to its consumption.[11]

Similar scenes unfolded across the United States, where government agents became suspicious of companies for using hempseed in their products. That same year, a manager of the feed department for the Philadelphia Seed Company sent a letter to the Department of Agriculture in Washington, DC,

Advertisement for the Philadelphia Seed Company, *c.* 1935.

claiming that the company's 'distributors in New Orleans received a rather threatening letter ... in which it is alleged that the Hemp Seed has been analysed and has been found to be a derivative of the plant known as Marihuana'. The agent who brought the news warned that 'this last named plant is used to manufacture some sort of dope', which confused the manager, so he decided to write to him, 'to determine if you can throw any light on this matter'.[12]

In 1937 the United States passed the Marihuana Tax Act, which placed such a burden upon hemp in the country that nobody wanted to grow it. However, a shortage of naval stores during the Second World War left the United States scrambling to reverse course. When Japan cut off their supply of plant-fibre imports from the Philippines, the Department of Agriculture created a film that called for all 'patriotic farmers' to take up cannabis cultivation so the government could 'meet the needs of our army and navy, as well as our industries'. In it, a scene showed a large bag of hempseed, which the narrator warned viewers to 'be careful how you use it'.[13] The film also claimed that 14,568 hectares' (36,000 ac) worth of hempseed were cultivated under the 'Hemp for Victory' programme the government established in 1942, less than half of which ended up being harvested for naval stores. The following year, they planned to expand that number to 20,234 hectares (50,000 ac).

The campaign was short-lived. The Marihuana Tax Act caused irreparable damage to the seed supply-line, and fibre imports through the Pacific were restored towards the end of the war. The U.S. government did cultivate more acreage in 1943 than ever before, but everything slid downhill from there. By the 1950s all parts of the plant were illegal to produce in the country, and perceptions of hempseed were more associated with what had become known as the noxious, foreign intoxicant

Poster for *Hemp for Victory* (1942), a short propaganda film by the U.S. Department of Agriculture.

called 'marihuana'. Subcultural segments of societies throughout the Atlantic world kept cannabis around as it transformed into a symbol of transnational countercultural identity, but hempseed as a food item went dormant until the hemp health movement restored its reputation.

Hempseed's Resurgence

After the 'Hemp for Victory' programme, public knowledge of the plant's multi-purpose use value in the United States dissipated. The film itself was buried in the archives and forgotten about until the 1980s, when author Jack Herer came across it. Herer, who had gravitated towards cannabis in the late 1960s at the age of thirty, is the author of a book that his acolytes call the 'hemp bible'.[14] Before then, the only thing he claimed to know about it came from the Reefer Madness campaign that dominated the discourse when he was younger. Even those who were well connected within the countercultural movement before he joined didn't seem to know much about the seed's value as a food source. Instead, they associated it with a sprout that eventually grew into the drug they used to signify their transgressive, anti-establishment identity. Herer's hunt to revive the plant's image, however, brought him into contact with sources that described hemp's historical value and potential across a range of industries, which he enthusiastically outlined in his widely popular book *The Emperor Wears No Clothes* (1985).

In the book, he vowed that hemp could save the world and raved about its fibre's potential to transform a host of businesses, the seeds' capacity to cure hunger and the buds' ability to heal humanity. The book is a highly sensationalized, conspiratorial narrative that often distorts the historical record through a selective reading of complex sources, but it grabbed people's attention and improved perceptions of the plant. In 1989 *High Times* published an article about his work that highlighted how 'Hemp seed is one of the world's best and cheapest sources of protein.'[15] The hemp health movement had begun, and the magazine credited Herer for spawning it. Ed Rosenthal did too, dedicating one of his edited volumes 'to Jack Herer, the founder of the modern hemp movement'. A contributing author

Poster by George Goode of Johnny Potseed, 1969, a countercultural mythological figure who went about planting cannabis seeds wherever he went.

in one of the chapters even held Herer responsible for the 'resurgence of interest in using hemp seeds for human nutrition in the United States and Western Europe'.[16]

High Times had a multinational readership by then, so his ideas reached a global audience. A couple of German restaurant owners published a hemp cookbook in 1999 that credited Herer for having 'presented for the first time the history of hemp prohibition and the people behind it, as well as the ... possibilities offered by [it] as a viable crop'. They continued: 'Years ago, encouraged by Herer's book, we began developing dishes made with hemp in the kitchen of our restaurant.'[17] In

Bowl of fruit and hempseed.

Tomato and peach hempseed salad.

another book, published in 2000, self-described 'HEMPSTER' Todd Dalotto claimed that Herer's book inspired him to 'synchronize my talents as a healing food-crafter, an activist, and an Earth caretaker'. He started Hungry Bear Hemp Foods in 1994, based out of Oregon, which sold products such as 'candy bars called *Seedy Sweeties*'. His book sought to 'inspire you, as I have been inspired, to improve the health of the planet and each other by making the best use of the hempseed'.[18]

Operating a business like that in the 1990s was difficult, since hempseed had only just begun to resurface as a food option in the United States after decades of prohibition. It was still illegal to cultivate cannabis for any reason, so Dalotto had to import the seeds to make his products. During the early days of Reefer Madness, the government reached an agreement with birdseed lobbyists that allowed companies to use hempseed in their products if the seeds were sterilized first. The process was time consuming and cost prohibitive, however, which led hemp foodies to form the Hemp Food Association (HFA) in 1998. All hemp cultivation remained illegal in the United States until 2018, but its food advocates during the late twentieth century paved the way for new culinary cultures to form around the seeds.

Dalotto's book, for example, included nearly two hundred pages of text filled with a variety of recipes. Desserts such as 'Hemp Nutty Cookies' and 'Vegan Hemp Raspberry Cheesecake' were included, as well as 'Hempseed Oil Nutty Avocado Salad' and 'Vegan Hempseed Stuffed Shells'. He also had some 'Baked Beets with Yogurt and Hempseed Oil' to offer, as well as a 'Porta-Rella Burger' that included a recipe for cheese derived from hempseed. This new-found praise for hempseed became so powerful that enthusiasts forgot all about the historical reluctance to consume it before the hemp health movement brought the plant's image back to life.

In fact, the author who credited Herer in that chapter of Rosenthal's edited book even went so far as to claim about its history that 'whenever hemp was cultivated, the nutritious and delicious seeds of the plant were prized as a food.'[19] This historical revisionism reveals how an unappealing food in one context can become more alluring or tasteful in another. For cannabis, the plant's association with countercultural identities helped people reimagine its seed consumption as a tasty, health-conscious choice, and this image has continued to rise in popularity alongside the psychoactive preparations people consume. Combined, they have drastically transformed the cultural meaning and significance behind eating cannabis.

Shiva enraged by Parvati's interruption of his meditation, early 19th century, painting from the Punjab Hills of northern India.

4
Eating Cannabis

Marijuana is meant to be eaten.
David Bienenstock, *The Official High Times Pot Smoker's Handbook* (2008)

An entire book could be written about the different preparations of cannabis for consumption in world history. Parts of the plant have been baked into sweets, infused into meals, extracted into consumable concentrates and ingested in a variety of forms. Historically this has usually been done by people seeking to alter their state of consciousness or provide their body with a dose of medicine. Increasingly as of late, however, arguments have been made in favour of eating cannabis as part of a healthy diet – and not just in the form of hempseed, either. Some are even presenting evidence on the benefits behind eating raw cannabis, straight off the live plant.

Back in 2005, before ever hearing of such a thing as eating raw cannabis, I was travelling across Russia on a cultural exchange programme. In the city of Volzhsky, our group met with members of a youth organization called Rotarak. At one of our meals, my travelling companion Brian Farda and I ended up in a conversation with a teenager named Misha that somehow made its way on to the topic of cannabis. I didn't know much about the plant then, so the best I could do was offer some commentary on how people smoked it in the United States.

Misha, however, mentioned that it grew everywhere in the Russian countryside, but that most plants did not to have any psychoactive effects when consumed.

None of us knew anything about cannabinoid profiles or genetic variabilities between cultivars, or else we could have explained the variation he described in these feral plants, but what really surprised me about that conservation – and why I bring it up now – is that Misha said he and his friends would occasionally pull the buds straight off the live plants and eat them. He couldn't quite explain what effect this had when I asked, but I was curious to see an example. Shortly after starting the search for a sample, however, we were informed by the rest of our group that it was time to leave for our next destination.

Years went by before I thought about this conversation again. But coming across articles on the potential benefits of eating raw cannabis brought the memory back to my mind.[1] Since then I've often wondered how many Russians shared Misha's consumption practice. Not much about it exists in the available literature on cannabis culture in Russia during the twentieth century, but that's understandable given how harshly the government penalized those who consumed it during the Soviet and post-Soviet eras. Academics such as Vera Rubin and others who contributed to *Cannabis and Culture* (1975) discussed aspects of folk cultures in eastern Europe and Russia that were connected to cannabis, but none of them specifically identified the practice of pinching off a cannabis flower from a ripening plant to eat.

One reference that hints about such a consumption practice comes from a hypothetical scenario that Robert C. Clarke and Mark D. Merlin concocted for their book *Cannabis: Evolution and Ethnobotany* (2013). In it they suggest that ancient man would have considered the 'ripe seeds' a 'worthwhile food'.[2] However, forty years earlier, Merlin included in one of his first books a strikingly similar hypothetical scenario, only back then he emphasized the 'resin-covered leaves' that ancient man 'enjoyed and revered [for] psychoactive use' as the primary purpose of their consumption.[3]

What changed during the period between both publications? Well, for one, the hemp health movement that Herer's hyperbolic 'revelations' sparked in the 1990s provided a new narrative for cannabis enthusiasts to use in their quest to rehabilitate the plant's reputation. Robyn Griggs Lawrence's *Pot in Pans* (2019) seems to take this approach by emphasizing that 'cavepeople' ate raw cannabis, which she describes as a 'nutritional powerhouse that has been largely ignored since humans discovered that heating the flowers or . . . extracting the plant's resin heightens its psychoactive and therapeutic effects'.[4]

In the end, we will likely never know what initially caused early humans to gravitate towards cannabis, but historical references do provide hints from Hinduism that allude to the plant being eaten raw somewhere around 3,500 years ago. According to many interpretations of the Vedic texts, for example, cannabis is one of the five sacred plants listed in the ancient scriptures. One of the three main Hindu gods, Lord Shiva, was said to have grown fond of it one day after storming out of a heated argument with his wife, Parvati. As one version of the story goes, he retreated into the Himalayan mountains in a fit of rage, eventually falling asleep underneath some trees near cannabis plants. When Shiva awoke from his slumber, he found himself in a powerful state of hunger, so he ate some of the cannabis leaves, which soothed his stomach and improved his mood. He has remained attached to the plant ever since.

Exactly when the first reference to cannabis emerges in ancient Sanskrit sources is still debated, but strong cultural ties to cannabis consumption in India can be accurately traced back far enough to indicate its important role as one of the first

Live cannabis flowering cluster (cola).

multi-purpose agricultural crops of significance in societies across the subcontinent more broadly. From there, it migrated up towards Central Asia and developed more variation as it dispersed through different climates and adapted over millennia. How much of it was eaten raw is hard to say, but once people discovered its psychoactive effects and started consuming it to alter their states of consciousness, a few preparations emerged across cultures that have stood the test of time.

Hashish, Majoun and Dawamesk

When it comes to the most widely referenced preparation of drug cannabis that people have eaten throughout history, hashish is the most ubiquitous. Majoun and dawamesk might have been more popular than hashish in specific areas at different times, but hashish is older and more widely known across different cultures. Majoun and dawamesk are also more like edible preparations containing some form of hashish as an ingredient, whereas hashish itself refers to variations of cannabis trichomes with psychoactive cannabinoids that have been separated from the rest of the plant. In India it's called 'charas', and in the Middle East and North Africa people often refer to it as 'kif'. Preparing cannabis into this concentrated form makes transporting it more efficient by reducing the amount of plant material one needs to carry (and consume) to obtain the desired effects.

One of the most significant stories about hashish in world history has been linked to Marco Polo, whose famous travel narrative included a vignette about an old man in the mountains of Persia who led a group of Shia Muslims called the Nizari Ismailis. According to legend, he coaxed his disciples into assassinating political rivals by giving them doses of a euphoric drug and promising them more in the afterlife. The story began as a fantastical exaggeration that has only magnified over the

A form of hashish.

centuries. France has been a particularly strong source of the tale, where Polo's book first appeared in 1355. Numerous editions and reprints followed, but in 1809 a European Orientalist named Antoine Isaac Silvestre de Sacy connected hashish to the story of the old man. Modern scholarship identifies him as 'Ala' al-Din Muhammad (d. 1255), the Imam of the Ismaili Muslims, who ruled from Alamut in Persia, but the lecture Sacy delivered that year in Paris titled 'Dynasty of Assassins and the Etymology of Their Name' had a lasting impact by claiming an etymological connection between the words *hachichin* and these 'assassins'.[5]

By then, French knowledge of drug cannabis had become infused with the exoticized lens of Orientalism, and Sacy had already devoted sections of previous publications to describing 'the hashish-eating dregs of society' scattered throughout the Arab world.[6] However, this lecture firmly codified the link between cannabis, Islam and violence within French society and the European imagination more broadly, having appeared in numerous publications and many languages ever since it came out. Relying on Sunni sources to selectively highlight prohibitionary measures against the drug while ignoring the nuanced complexity behind the history of cannabis in Asia and Africa, Sacy condemned the plant as a representation of Oriental degeneracy. By doing so, he magnified the dichotomy of difference between Eastern and Western uses that had been metastasizing for decades.

His condemnation also came at a time when Western medical practitioners were studying chemistry more closely. One such practitioner was William Brooke O'Shaughnessy, who served as a chemist and colonial doctor for the British East India Company (EIC) in the 1830s. At the Medical College of Calcutta, he tapped into the vast array of indigenous knowledge that Hindus, Muslims, Indians and Persians had developed on cannabis over the centuries. He also relied on Sacy and described the 'dregs of the populace' who were 'dissipated and depraved' as they indulged in a 'debauch' of consumption that 'leads [them] to madness'.[7] After regurgitating the assassin's legend and engaging in the type of Orientalist-infused discourse that often appeared in medical publications such as the one he produced in 1839, O'Shaughnessy elaborated on the benefits that his more 'civilized' extraction of the plant had to offer. Excerpts from his pamphlet were disseminated widely across the Atlantic world, popularizing his preparation and increasing demand for medicinal cannabis extracts across Europe and the Americas.

His praise and condemnation for cannabis wasn't unique. Instead, it reflects the duality of Orientalism described earlier that both repulsed and attracted the Western mind, which also influenced the French pharmacists and doctors who tried to tame cannabis in the decades after Sacy's lecture.[8] By the 1840s one of those doctors, Jacques-Joseph Moreau de Tours, formed the Club des Hashischins so he could study mental illness by observing the drug's effects on the artists, students and literary figures who attended the meetings. One of the participants described how Moreau presided over the consumption ceremony in Eastern garb to resemble the 'Old Man of the Mountain' as he administered a 'green paste' to the guests so they could 'taste the joys of the paradise of Muhammad'.[9] It's as if Sacy's myth, which both proponents and opponents of the club's activities referenced, served as one of the placebo texts through which they came to understand the drug.

In fact, the legend followed cannabis around throughout French society, even causing some to question the safety of cultivating it for hemp fibre. Many also touted its medical potential while warning of its sinister effects, but all referred to its Middle Eastern connections to madness and the old man's assassins. The curiosity of those who participated in playing Eastern with Moreau by eating cannabis at the club meetings, however, was

The Old Man of the Mountain ('Ala' al-Din Muhammad) drugging his disciples, mid-13th century, miniature from an illustrated edition of Marco Polo, *Le Livre des merveilles*, c. 1400.

based off the more attractive elements of Orientalism. They romanticized hashish as a symbol of otherness that they consumed to play out their Oriental fantasies and, by doing so, established one of the first well-documented developments of a European subculture ceremoniously eating parts of the plant as a recreational drug.

Something similar developed across the United States, where pharmacists at the time also touted its benefits and orientalized its dangers. The practice of playing Eastern was certainly informing U.S. medical knowledge of cannabis in 1859, when a group of doctors called the American Provers' Union published a pamphlet titled *Provings of Cannabis Indica*. Their understanding of the medicine relied on the work of Bayard Taylor, whose reputation as a public performer of Orientalism expanded when *Putnam's Magazine* published his article 'Visions of Hasheesh' in 1854. In it, Taylor described vivid hallucinations revolving around the terrors and pleasures he experienced after consuming the drug in Damascus. The story intensified the placebo text of Orientalism that the provers and others like them used to develop their medical understanding of the plant.

The infusion of Orientalism into the medical discourse on cannabis can also be seen in Fitz Hugh Ludlow's *The Hasheesh Eater* (1857). It's a lurid tale about his experiences eating the drug for a period of months that weaves Orientalist allure into a narrative about the tantalizing terrors that the drug supposedly generated in him. Early in the text he describes going to an apothecary and stumbling upon a bottle of 'Cannabis indica', which the owner warned was both a medicine and a 'deadly poison'.[10] This intrigued the self-proclaimed 'pharmaceutical Alexander', so he searched the transatlantic trail of publications and discovered that it derived from the same plant that was 'the subject of a most graphic chapter from the pen of Bayard Taylor', which moved him 'powerfully to curiosity and admiration'. From then on, he referred to the medicine as 'Hasheesh', thereby further blurring the line between medical and literary representations of cannabis consumption.[11]

Thomas Hicks, *Bayard Taylor*, 1855, oil on canvas.

The book had a broad audience and went through several editions, with more than a few reviews appearing on both sides of the Atlantic. Most were quite critical, with one reviewer warning readers not to imitate his use of this 'drug of enchantment' because it 'is one of the most fatal of all diabolic illusions' and has become a 'habitual indulgence with all classes of society in India, Persia, and Turkey'. Another called Ludlow a foolish 'Transatlantic Pythagorean' who seemed willing 'to adopt anything, from a creed to a medicine'. Someone else complained that his 'imitation of Oriental habits' was the biggest problem because 'the Caucasian races, no longer content with tobacco, coffee, and tea, are beginning to crave and use the stronger narcotics.'[12] The fear of a menacing form of Oriental intoxication pervading and contaminating Western civilization was transforming cannabis into a highly contested plant.

Yet simultaneously, Orientalism continued to inspire a transatlantic subculture of consumption, as seen in the life and works of an eccentric man named Paschal Beverly Randolph. He grew up as an orphan in the slums of New York City at a time when many African Americans faced some form of oppressive servitude, but Randolph was born free. By his mid-thirties, he had become a rather accomplished author of publications on occult philosophies and a known supporter of early feminism who delivered charismatic lectures to large audiences. Randolph also completed three separate voyages across the Atlantic that included time spent in the UK, France, Spain, Greece, Egypt and several regions of Asia Minor. He claimed to have first encountered cannabis while visiting 'mesmerists' in France, but that 'in Egypt I studied it perfectly'.[13] When he returned to the United States, he brought some back with him.

Like Taylor, Randolph began playing Eastern with hashish upon his return. He claimed the drug could induce a mental state called 'clairvoyance', a form of seership where 'the mind, leaping all the barriers of the outer senses and world, sees and knows things altogether beyond their ranges'. He sometimes called it 'Dowameskh' or 'Oriental hemp', and he purportedly administered the drug to more than six hundred patients without issue. In advertisements for his services, however, Randolph warned potential consumers to watch out for imposters selling inferior products that were incapable of producing the 'extasia' and 'fantasia' of hashish because they didn't come from a genuine, 'Oriental' source the way his preparations did.[14] A fair number of people must have listened to his claims, for he self-published dozens of manuscripts, circulated numerous advertisements and gave plenty of presentations.

By the 1870s, however, Randolph's reputation as a hashish-eating 'sex-magician' with ideas from the fringes of society brought public accusations of insanity against him.[15] He eventually changed his mind about the drug, referring to it in 1871 as a 'curse' that 'carries misfortune wherever 'tis seen'.[16] Some said he committed suicide in 1875, but others have disputed that claim. Still, Ludlow had already died young by then, the circumstances of which some blamed on a life filled with Oriental indulgence, and the notion of drug addiction as a major menace to Western civilization was on the rise. The plant was falling out of favour fast, yet still people such as the occultists Helena Blavatsky and Albert Rawson gravitated towards its use. More countries might have been moving towards a culture of fear and restriction when it came to cannabis, but subcultures continued to embrace the plant for what its drug properties came to symbolize in their societies.

Something similar unfolded in the UK and Germany. Those seeking liberation from the constraints of Victorian culture embraced cannabis consumption and drug use more broadly. Not only that, but the more consumption became associated with degeneration and cultural deterioration, the more attractive

Dr. P. B. Randolph's Great Pamphlets.

The Unveiling of Spiritualism!

This is a minute detail of the singular experience of Dr. Randolph, (the famous converted medium,) and settles the question about Spiritualism most effectually. Its description of the Devil and God, at a game of Chess is one of the most thrilling things in the language. Price 25 cents, post paid.

ALSO,

BY THE SAME AUTHOR,

Human Love,

IN ITS PHYSICAL ASPECTS,

HOW IT IS MADE SICK, AND HOW CURED.

It also contains one single piece of information, called "THE GRAND SECRET," alone worth fifty times the cost. Price 25 cents. Also, "THE GOLDEN LETTER," 25 cents.

Address, N. E. REFORM ASSOCIATION,

BOSTON MASS.

Advertisement for Paschal Beverly Randolph's pamphlets, 'The Unveiling of Spiritualism!' and 'Human Love', 1861.

it became. The British poet Arthur Symons called this 'the decadent movement', which inspired literary figures such as Aleister Crowley and others to use hashish in their exploration of consciousness. Crowley even became known as a 'Wizard of Wickedness' and the 'King of Depravity', and the German philosopher Walter Benjamin labelled his experiments eating hashish from 1927 to 1934 as 'profane illumination'.[17] The Beat Generation drew tremendous influence from this theme as well, which laid the foundation for a transatlantic movement to emerge that shifted the meaning of cannabis more strongly towards a symbol of transgressive cultural identity.

Countercultural Consumption

The bond between drug consumption and transgressive identity strengthened within middle-class cultures during the first half of the twentieth century. Inhaling cannabis replaced ingesting it as the primary route of administration, partly because smoking drastically reduces the time it takes for cannabinoids to enter the bloodstream. When cannabis is eaten, the cannabinoids must be broken down through the digestive system before they can metabolize in the liver and enter the bloodstream, which takes anywhere from thirty minutes to a couple of hours, depending on what the person ate beforehand and how their body functions. The effects are more potent and unpredictable as well, whereas the effects of smoking are felt instantly and are much easier to titrate (determine dosage). These factors made smokable preparations of the plant more appealing to labourers who used them for relief or restorative purposes, which became a well-established cultural practice in regions across Mesoamerica, Asia, Africa and the diaspora communities derived from them in societies around the world.

Jazz culture also contributed to the shift towards smoking cannabis. Musicians such as Billie Holiday, Louis Armstrong, Dizzy Gillespie, Mezz Mezzrow, John Dankworth and Django Reinhardt made it fashionable to smoke what many called 'tea', 'muggles' or 'reefer'. Cab Calloway's song 'Reefer Man' (1932) and the popular song from the Mexican Revolution 'La Cucaracha' (1910s) provide insight into patterns of consumption within the marginalized communities that gravitated towards smoking marijuana. The British started describing smokable cannabis as marijuana at this time as well, where an even longer historical tradition of associating such modes of consumption with colonized people was already well established. The situation was similar for the French, too, who continued connecting cannabis to Islam and violence as the African-originated custom of smoking surpassed the popularity of eating drug preparations of the plant.

This added an element of appeal to the drug for nonconformists who started calling themselves the Beats after the international dust from the Second World War began to settle. Their fascination with how 'the other half lived', so to speak, served a similar function to Orientalism for writers like Taylor and Ludlow in the nineteenth century, who were drawn towards cannabis as a thrillingly 'otherizing' substance. The excitement these authors, poets and playwrights experienced as they frequented Black night clubs and soaked in the stories of life that jazz music offered was intoxicating. It invested cannabis with a new meaning for them; one that fed into their rejection of the conformity culture in the 1950s.

Despite these subcultural trends, however, the UN sent a clear message about the 'proper' stance that civilized nations were expected to take towards drug consumption. Fears of people 'running amok' had already caused the League of Nations to focus more on suppressing cannabis in the 1930s,

Poster for Cab Calloway's 'Have You Ever Met That Funny Reefer Man', *c.* 1932, composed by J. Russel Robinson with lyrics by Andy Razaf.

but the UN's Single Convention on Narcotic Drugs in 1961 established a firmer international system of control over the cultivation, production, distribution and definition of the proper use for certain drugs. The foundation upon which a global war against consumption was set, with more draconian measures implemented in the ensuing decades. Even today, as cannabis laws within some member states shift away from the UN's global model, the International Narcotics Control Board (INCB) warns of increased trafficking and deleterious ramifications for those contravening the position outlined in the Single Convention.

Against the backdrop of this global war, a transnational resistance movement emerged to challenge it. As the unconventional interests of the Beats blossomed into a countercultural movement in the 1960s, more young adults and college students adopted cannabis as a symbol of anti-establishment attitudes against institutionalized authority. Demand for the drug increased, so people started thinking of new ways to secure a supply. One pathway that emerged became known as the Hashish Trail. It started in Europe, wound through Turkey and Iran, then continued east to Bangkok. At one point, it served as a rite of passage for those who embraced the countercultural lifestyle, but eventually turned into a popular tourist-type destination that helped place the concept of eating cannabis back on the menu as a fashionable mode of consumption.

Legal hashish shop in Kathmandu, 1973.

A few years before this provocative pathway became part of a countercultural pilgrimage, one of the most important publications connected to the re-emergence of eating cannabis as a popular form of consumption appeared in the United States and the UK. *The Alice B. Toklas Cook Book* (1954) has become a cult classic for cannabis enthusiasts, but the 77-year-old American-born expatriate who wrote it did not live long enough to see its rise to fame. For decades before the book came out, Toklas had been living in Paris with her life partner, writer Gertrude Stein, but following Stein's death in 1946, her family was able to confiscate the couple's valuable assets, since they were not legally married. This left Toklas in a state of financial ruin and desperate for some income, so she asked her friends for a few recipes to include in a cookbook she planned to publish.

One of those friends was the British Canadian Beat artist and writer Brion Gysin, who was living in Morocco. The recipe he sent her, titled 'Haschich Fudge', is why the book eventually became so famous. He described it as the 'food of Paradise – of Baudelaire's Artificial Paradises' and promised it would 'provide an entertaining refreshment' with 'brilliant storms of laughter' and 'ecstatic reveries'. He described the recipe as a 'bunch of canibus [*sic*] sativa' that was 'pulverized' and 'kneaded together' with a bunch of other ingredients. According to an interview Toklas gave after the book came out, she wasn't aware that 'hashish was the accented part of the recipe'.[18] The editors at Harper & Brothers certainly recognized the ingredient, which caused them to remove it from the first U.S. edition. The British edition did include the recipe, however, as have subsequent U.S. editions since the 1960s.

Despite Toklas's unfamiliarity with the controversial ingredient, her name became forever connected to cannabis and the countercultural movement. As if the cookbook wasn't enough,

Brazilian brigadeiros.

one of the Hashish Trail travellers solidified this connection when he released the countercultural film *I Love You, Alice B. Toklas* (1968). In the script, the Haschich Fudge of her cookbook was replaced with cannabis-infused brownies. Since then, they have been referred to by such names as canna-brownies, special brownies, groovy brownies, wownies, pot or weed brownies and space cakes. Unfortunately, Toklas never lived to see the distortions by which her name made it to the big screen, for she died a year before the film was released. The canna-brownie, however, lived on to become the most iconic form of eating cannabis in countercultural history, which has inspired similar such confections around the world.

One woman who became famous for making cannabis brownies was Mary Jane Rathbun. The historian Emily Dufton referred to her as the 'Florence Nightingale of Medical Marijuana' because of her unwavering commitment to providing HIV and AIDS patients in the Castro District of San Francisco with access to the medicine, which significantly increased their quality of life while battling the disease.[19] She also helped transform perceptions of cannabis consumption in the same way that Nightingale transformed perceptions of nursing. By the late 1970s she had affectionately become known as 'Brownie Mary' among her (much younger) community of friends. After being arrested in 1981 with enough cannabis to send her to prison for a very long time, some say her race (white), motherly persona and kind disposition got most of the charges dropped; she did end up serving five hundred hours of community service, however.

This is when Rathbun really started to merge her countercultural lifestyle with a new-found passion for volunteerism. In 1983 she joined the Shanti Project, which provides support services to people struggling with terminal illnesses. The patients who took her cannabis-infused brownies overwhelmingly reported regaining an appetite, experiencing pain relief and becoming more active in their daily lives. She became a habitual and award-winning volunteer at the San Francisco General Hospital before being arrested again in 1992, when the police raided a friend's home while Rathbun was inside baking brownies with 1 kilogram (2 lb) of cannabis. She had been giving them away for free since the time of her first arrest, but police still charged her with possession and intent to sell. Once again, however – albeit after much stress and struggle fighting the conviction – the charges were dropped.

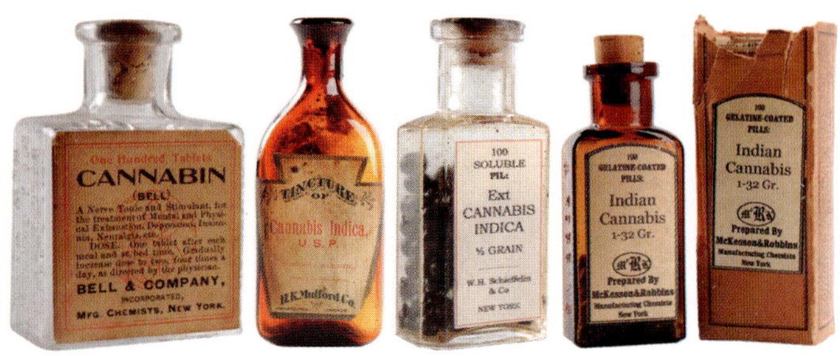

Cannabis tinctures and medicines from the 19th and early 20th centuries in the United States.

By then Rathbun was 68 years old and well prepared to argue for her defence at trial, which transformed her into a celebrity. She used this new-found fame to appear on talk shows and give interviews with news outlets across the country to shed light on the value of medical cannabis use. Her efforts presented a compassionate point of view that remedicalized the drug's image and contributed to California passing Proposition 215 in 1996, which recognized a patient's right to consume it. Just like that, California became the first U.S. state to relegalize the plant for medical purposes. Others soon followed, but the country remained divided on what forms of consumption, if any, should be legitimized. Recreational use remained banned everywhere until the next century, but more people were paying attention to its medicinal properties.

Distinguishing between recreational and medical cannabis consumption, however, can be problematic. One could, for example, not realize that their consumption serves a medical purpose, or conversely convince themselves that something is therapeutic when it causes harm. There could also be medicines with unsafe ingredients that contain no benefits at all. The point is that consumption cannot be separated from the cultural setting in which it occurs and the psychological state of the consumer. What seems recreational in one setting could be therapeutic in another, and recreational consumption might even be a form of medicine for some. Moreover, one culture may interpret recreational consumption as a representation of degeneracy, while another might not even recognize such cultural forms of use. Culture invests meaning into the things people use and do, which significantly shapes societal perceptions of them.

The World Health Organization (WHO) might have declared cannabis completely devoid of medical value by the 1960s, for example, but marginalized populations persisted in using it as a therapeutic tool. Trauma, hunger, pain and social and emotional exhaustion are all aspects of life that cannabis can help alleviate, and which oppressed peoples experience disproportionately more than others.

When the social-code breakers of the 1950s began embracing elements of marginalized cultures, however, new meanings were woven into the fabric of cannabis consumption. The plant transformed into a symbol of transgressive cultural identity in the ensuing decades, even as global governments started

Space cakes from Amsterdam, 2007.

escalating their control efforts and cracking down on distribution networks in the 1970s. A transnational movement against this criminalization developed to try and relegitimize its use, but the mechanisms of control suppressed it, alongside the growing body of knowledge pertaining to cannabis's medical value. All the while, its popularity as a countercultural symbol continued to intensify.

It was at this time the Netherlands became known as a haven for those seeking refuge from the increasingly harsher laws of prohibition, even if the plant officially remained illegal there. The Dutch granted licences permitting cannabis to be sold and consumed in coffee shops starting in the 1970s, but these storefronts had to be discreet in their operations. By the mid-1980s hundreds were open in cities across the country. The numbers kept climbing until the Dutch passed laws regulating and limiting their capacity in the 1990s, but there are still nearly two hundred of them open across the country today. One of the signature products for sale in these coffee shops is

Reefer's Bay cannabis cereal bar.

Caramel cannabis edible, Oregon, 2016.

the edible confection known as space cakes, which has become Amsterdam's version of the cannabis brownie.

Space cakes started out as square-shaped baked goods that were infused with cannabis. The earliest reference to them appeared in Amsterdam's first coffee shop, which opened back in 1972, the Mellow Yellow. Since then, space cakes have evolved into an iconic symbol of cannabis culture worldwide, on par with the brownie. Transgressive countercultural consumption kept these products relatively basic, but after the modern medical marijuana and recreational use movements developed into more legitimately recognized industries, the variability and diversity of edible cannabis options expanded drastically. Space cakes and brownies gave way to cannabis cookies, truffles and sugary sweet assortments of all kinds. Since chocolate is known as one of the most palatable pairings for cannabis, a slew of sweets became popular options – ranging from cannabis-infused chocolate bars to chocolate pretzel bites. Gummies, lollipops and hard cannabis sweets have also become popular consumable options, as well as cannabis snacks such as popcorn, crisps and all sorts of processed foods.

The rapid expansion of edible cannabis products over the past decade reflects how the plant is shifting towards a more acceptable position within societies whose governments have spent decades waging war against its use. Although it remains under strict control in most countries, decriminalization, recreational and medicalization movements keep gaining momentum. Only time will tell where they lead.

5
Drinking Cannabis

> A glass in the morning is guaranteed to relieve symptoms
> and leave a pleasant feeling that lasts all day.
>
> Dr Poppy's Wonder Elixir with Cannabis Extract

For Charlotte Figi, this quote from a mid-twentieth-century advertisement in Australia for a bottle of cannabis medicine wasn't a lie. She didn't consume her version in a glass, like Dr Poppy suggested around a half century earlier, but rather sublingually through a dropper that placed the liquid extract under her tongue. Actually, at first, her parents tried mixing it into her drinks once they discovered the anti-convulsant properties of CBD, but they soon realized that the 'under the tongue' method was more effective in reducing their daughter's seizures. This is because sublingual administration allows the body to absorb the medicine into its bloodstream more efficiently than gulping it down. There is a higher level of bioavailability when liquid extracts of cannabis rest under the tongue for a while, but the substance is still swallowed like a drink.

In 2009, before the CBD bonanza broke out, Charlotte was having multiple severe seizures per day that could not be controlled. Doctors diagnosed her with a debilitating form of epilepsy known as Dravet syndrome, but they could not reduce the frequency of her seizures. Despite trying all types of pharmaceutical medicines, she continued to suffer from hundreds of them each week. The family became desperate and was willing to try anything, which is how they met the Stanley Brothers, who owned a marijuana dispensary in Colorado. The plant became legal for medical use there in 2000, so the Figi family moved to Colorado Springs to seek help. After learning about their situation, the Stanley Brothers developed a cannabis cultivar so potent in CBD that an extract of it drastically reduced the number of Charlotte's seizures. They named it Charlotte's Web, and the Figi family credits it for transforming their lives.

Although Charlotte passed away in 2020, the cannabis medicine she consumed significantly improved the quality of

Dr Poppy's Wonder Elixir, 1946, enamel plate advertising.

her last seven years of life. By then, her mother, Paige, had become a strong advocate for access to the plant, which led people from across the United States to pay her a visit. Many of them stayed in the Figi household while they worked out how to secure a supply of the medicine for their own kids. These 'cannabis refugees', as one journalist described them, essentially fled to Colorado because the plant was still illegal where they lived in the United States.[1] They were being forced to choose between becoming criminals or passing over an opportunity to significantly help a loved one. For many, the choice was as obvious to them as it was to Paige, which meant that her home was frequently filled with guests.

Given the circumstances, one might say that there is a form of medical apartheid taking place when it comes to cannabis. People who need it for potentially life-threatening conditions are restricted from access based on where they live, and those who are arrested for possession are four times as likely to be a person of colour than they are white. The 1956 Narcotics Control Act in the United States made possession a crime punishable by up to ten years in prison and a $20,000 fine, yet the Federal Bureau of Narcotics (FBN) knew cannabis had the potential to alleviate symptoms of epilepsy. In 1949, for example, the FBN Commissioner, Harry Anslinger, sent memos through his department that contained clippings of articles discussing faculty researchers at the University of Utah who were working on a cure for epilepsy that included 'marijuana leaves' – and that's just scratching the surface.[2] They had access to evidence going back decades, in fact, but still proceeded to criminalize.

Some sources even suggest that the plant's anti-convulsant properties were known in China, Egypt and India as far back as 2000 BCE. William Brooke O'Shaughnessy discussed it in his pamphlet from the 1830s, with subsequent medical journals repeating his claims as nineteenth-century physicians and medical professionals created a golden age for cannabis tinctures and elixirs. Liquid extracts of it became widespread pharmaceutical ingredients throughout the Atlantic World during this period, but the global drug war brought an end to it in the 1950s. Well before any of these products existed, however, one historical form of drinking cannabis stands out the most for its ties to culturally significant customs across Asia.

Bhang

As mentioned earlier, the word 'bhang' has multiple meanings in reference to cannabis. Cognates of it from multiple languages have been used generically to describe other types of drugs, but it also refers to a drinkable preparation that includes ground-up leaves and plant matter as an ingredient. In Western sources, the term is often used in reference to the traditional Indian drinks *bhang lassi* and *bhang thandai*. The Bengali word *siddhi* has also been used to describe the beverage, which is one of the oldest preparations of the plant in world history. As a cultural custom, it seems to have also dispersed along the Silk Road. At some point, people living around the Hindu Kush mountain range incorporated it into the ceremonial beverages they prepared for use in their religious practices and cosmologies.

Exactly when this began is hard to tell. Ancient Egyptian texts as well as the Rig Veda (1500s BCE), Atharva Veda (1000s BCE), Zend Avesta (700s BCE) and the Torah (700s BCE) are some of the commonly cited references, but issues of context and translation accuracy have caused doubts in some of the claims. Hem Chunder Kerr's report from the 1870s claims it derived from the Sanskrit *bhanga* in the Atharva Veda. Since *bhanga* stems from the root word 'to break', he argued that it

Man preparing bhang, Turkmenistan, 1865–72.

referred to cannabis used for fibre, but that its medicinal qualities were also known. The beverage had certainly become a well-established form of consumption across the subcontinent by the time the British began their 'civilizing mission' in India. Smoking ganja and consuming charas were described as deplorable acts, but drinking bhang was more acceptable.

Just over two decades later, the Indian Hemp Drugs Commission (IHDC) parroted this perception, albeit with a slightly softer tone. The 1,189 'witnesses' across British India who were interviewed for the commission provided ample data to analyse the role that cannabis drugs played in the subcontinent, but it wasn't exactly objective. Most of the committee didn't call for prohibition, but their report (and most of its witnesses) viewed cannabis drugs through a colonial lens that asserted the legitimacy of modern medicine, imperial control and revenue accumulation over indigenous knowledge cultures. Their perception was predicated on what one drug scholar called the 'denial of value and validity of what colonists referred to as "local traditions" as opposed to modern science'.[3]

Of course, denying these 'local traditions' also meant rejecting what one scholar in 2022 referred to as India's 'polyvalent and relational notions of the experience of intoxication' that emphasized the role of 'variable contexts, specific social relations, and articulations of intention, deterrence, and discernment' when consuming cannabis.[4] The British supplanted these multidimensional, context-oriented and relationally specific forms of knowing drugs and replaced them with a singular, Eurocentric knowledge system that contained easily identifiable categories to label, regulate and control through taxation and policing. The IHDC achieved this goal by compiling 'evidence' that separated cannabis into three supposedly concrete categories for the colonial regime to codify into law: bhang, ganja and charas.

Veiled beneath this simplified typology was a complex understanding of consumption based on cultural context. In the history of proverbs about cannabis, for example, ganja and charas were not always represented as degenerate or deplorable, and bhang doesn't always appear as a benign intoxicant. In some cases, bhang and ganja aren't even considered separate categories, and devotional communities of Hindus paid homage to several deities by investing culturally specific meanings into bhang consumption. Other times, proverbs conveyed messages about caste distinctions or taught lessons about the consequences of overindulgence. Some contained coded forms of consumption, with warriors often consuming it before marching off to battle. The hot summers in parts of northern India made drinking bhang a popular form of cooling down as well. These nuanced, context-specific, relationally oriented meanings did not fit neatly into the British colonial model, so they dismissed and displaced them.

After independence (1947), the legacy of this colonial era typology lingered on. Bhang's status still varied significantly from region to region, but it remained the most acceptable form of consumption – so much so that India's delegation at the UN's Single Convention (1961) fought to remove parts of the plant from the definition of cannabis. It also influenced India's Narcotic Drugs and Psychotropic Substances (NDPS) Act of 1985, which came about after the United States became the leading nation in the global war against drug cultures. Eager not to lose

Preparation and consumption of bhang, Amritsar, *c.* 1870, gouache.

its eligibility for aid and to fulfil its obligations as a UN member-state, the Indian National Congress passed the NDPS Act to establish a stronger framework for controlling and policing internationally scheduled 'narcotics' such as cannabis.

Yet bhang continued to remain relevant in the religious practices and everyday life of many people across the country. An anthropologist conducting field work on *akharas* in the 1980s found that wrestlers who trained in the traditional arena associated bhang consumption with controlling sexual desires and calming and focusing the mind.[5] It was simply too relevant in various aspects of people's lives across the country to be condemned entirely, so the national government took a page from its colonial past by leaving out the seeds and leaves from the definition of cannabis, which – like the IHDC report – implied that bhang could not be as deleterious to consumers as ganja or charas. The NDPS Act also prohibited all forms of cannabis cultivation in India without a state-issued licence, which allowed approved bhang shops to operate within designated areas.

The Indian government has continued to maintain a firm grip over its production and distribution in the decades since, but there have been signs that a more lenient policy might be under way. In 2021 the UN removed the plant from its most stringent schedule of dangerous drugs, which opened the door for relegitimizing legalization movements among member states such as India.

Tinctures and Elixirs

Cannabis was well integrated into Western medicine by the time it was criminalized. Centuries earlier the Age of Exploration increased European encounters, with vague references to bhang, but those who mentioned it didn't know much. The

Government-authorized bhang shop, Jaisalmer, 2006.

Portuguese naturalist Garcia de Orta described it in 1563 as something that came from a plant that looked like European hemp but served a much different purpose. He mentioned how the 'juice' for drinking was 'expressed from the pounded leaves and sometimes also from the seeds' before being mixed with 'some nutmeg, some mace, sometimes cloves' to create a concoction that caused those who drank it to be 'ravished in ecstasy'.[6] His exoticized description of the drink is indicative of references that appeared over the next two-and-a-half centuries. Some called it 'Bangie' or 'Bidjia' and listed medical uses or recreational follies associated with its consumption, but they didn't have much understanding of the drink.

During the first quarter of the nineteenth century, however, innovations in pharmacology led to more interest in studying Eastern cannabis among European and U.S. medical practitioners. One of the earliest sources comes from Samuel Hahnemann, whose theory of homeopathy involved physicians trying out medicines on themselves and documenting their experiences. The American Provers' Union referenced his popular publication *Materia Medica Pura* (1830), as did O'Shaughnessy and those who cited his work during the 1840s and '50s. In it, Hahnemann included a list of experiments and observations from his 'provings' with cannabis, which he conducted using a mixture of 'the fresh expressed juice of the tops of the flowering male or female hemp-plant, mixed with equal parts alcohol'.[7]

When O'Shaughnessy started studying this 'fresh expressed juice' at the Medical College in Calcutta, he came across Persian and Hindu sources that provided extensive details. One of the scholars he referenced was someone named Ameer, who demonstrated how to make 'Majoon' and 'Bang' in front of him on several occasions – the recipes for which O'Shaughnessy provided in his 1839 pamphlet that circulated so widely throughout the Atlantic World. He claimed that a 'tincture of the Hemp leaf in wine or spirit' was considered the preferred method of consumption, however, for which he provided instructions on preparation. He also raved that the tincture was, among other benefits, an 'anti-convulsive remedy of the greatest value'.[8]

In 1841 O'Shaughnessy showed up in London with a supply of ganja from India, which he gave to a pharmacist. He also delivered lectures on its medicinal value to various societies during his stay. By mid-century, apothecaries and pharmaceutical companies across the Atlantic were selling it and other cannabis concoctions as remedies for all sorts of ailments. One of the U.S. manufacturers was Tilden & Co., which produced the extract that Fitz Hugh Ludlow found at his apothecary and started referring to as hashish. That's about when the golden age for cannabis tinctures emerged.[9] Elixirs were also prevalent, which mixed the plant extracts with a variety of substances. By the end of the nineteenth century, advertisements varied widely in the types of ailments they claimed to cure. Tetanus, neuralgia, insanity, insomnia, headaches, delirium tremens, urinary infections and menstrual cramps are just a few. Several brands of cough syrup containing cannabis were also widely marketed.

There weren't many restrictions on what companies could say about the efficacy of their medical products, so they contained exaggerated claims and overstated assertions. Physicians often complained about how erratic these medicines were, with some calling them poisonous because they caused panic attacks, reminiscent of rumours that the plant induced insanity. Others expressed disappointment over the lack of certainty with its effects. Robert Jackson, for example, complained about 'its exceeding uncertainty of action, small doses in some cases causing marked symptoms, whilst in other instances a full dose produce no effect'.[10] Chemists still hadn't isolated cannabinoids

Dr Shoop's Tonic, 20th century.

yet, so they didn't understand the diversity that existed between different cultivars at the molecular level. This hindered the ability of physicians to determine why some batches were too potent and others didn't work at all. Proper dosages were still difficult to determine well into the twentieth century, in fact, so preconceived notions of its sinister uses by nefarious people continued to loom over the plant's reputation like a dark cloud.

Yet cannabis tonics, tinctures and elixirs continued to circulate on some level or another into the 1950s, although they started declining significantly in the 1920s. Since alcohol was a primary ingredient in most of these substances, the Volstead Act that legislated its prohibition in the United States (1920–33) didn't help with access. Various Canadian provinces also had a series of alcohol prohibitions in the early twentieth century that likely stifled the supply of tinctures. Cannabis became a medicine there as well after word of O'Shaughnessy's experiments travelled across the Atlantic. The influential Canadian physician and medical scholar William Osler claimed that 'indica is probably the most satisfactory remedy for migraines and epilepsy.'[11] In the 1920s it fell under strict control there too, which slowly pushed cannabis tinctures out of mainstream medicine.

Alcohol prohibition ended in the United States in 1933, but Reefer Madness took its place. The culture war that criminalized cannabis in the ensuing decades caused these types of medicines to practically disappear, but consumers developed clandestine versions to replace them. One of them contains Everclear, a potent grain alcohol produced by American Distilling Company in the 1950s that is known for its very high alcohol content by volume (ABV). It's difficult to determine when people started using it to make their own tinctures, but an advertisement from *High Times* in April 1979 describes how it was 'getting rave reviews everywhere' by then. Thirty years

Tincture bottles, 19th century.

later, its use for such purposes remained strong: an article from the November 2013 edition provides a recipe for 'Green Dragon Jell-O shots' and claims 'Everclear is a favourite [ingredient]'.[12]

The reason this alcohol is so useful in creating homemade tinctures is because cannabinoids are highly soluble in alcohol, so they dissolve more effectively when high-proof spirits are used as a solvent in the extraction process. When cannabis is soaked in a glass or jar of Everclear for a few days or – according to some – a few weeks, its active drug compounds separate and disperse more efficiently throughout the liquid. The resulting tincture has little to no remaining alcohol content and can be mixed with other substances or heated up to burn off the residual solvent for a more refined concentrate. With cannabis prohibition on the rise and alcohol back on the market, people took advantage of the opportunity to create access through developing new modes of consumption.

Of course, none of these preparations were legal to make, sell or consume. Liquid forms of synthetic THC produced by pharmaceutical companies, which have been around since the 1980s, eventually were, however. One of them was called Syntex Marinol solution, and several countries still have versions for sale today. Sativex is another, which GW Pharmaceuticals developed in 2010 as an oral spray that includes both THC and CBD cannabinoids; Canada, the United States, Spain, Germany, Australia and the UK still allow the regulated sale of it. A pure CBD version named Epidiolex emerged a few years later, but medical cannabis experts often describe it and others as inferior products because they lack the entourage effect described in Chapter Two.

Other solvents such as naphtha, butane or hexane are used to extract cannabinoids as well, but doing so can be dangerous, particularly if low-grade equipment is used and fire-hazard precautions aren't taken. With so many new extraction processes

CBD oil.

and tincture combinations hitting the market today, however, after all those years of criminalization, it appears that another golden age is in the making.

Cannabis Cocktails

By the time cannabis medicines were being removed from the shelves and the Beats were becoming trailblazers towards the east, cultural exchanges between cannabis consumers were causing new forms of consumption to appear in Western cultures.

Shennong, 19th century, watercolour.

The Australian traveller Richard Neville described encountering bhang in Afghanistan for the first time during the 1960s, and investigative journalist Peter Gorman mentioned coming across it in Nepal and India a couple of decades later. The British travel writer Colin Thubron's book *Shadow of the Silk Road* describes a cannabis drink he encountered along the well-worn route in the early 2000s. The Hashish Trail had already faded away by then, but Thubron followed its shadow into China, where he encountered a traditional cannabis drink called *ma cha* (麻茶). This 'hemp tea', some claim, rivals bhang as the oldest form of drinking cannabis in world history.

It's hard to know for sure, but one of the oldest written records to definitively mention drinking cannabis does come from China. The manuscript is titled *Pen Ts'ao Ching* and it appeared at some point during the Han Dynasty, but the list of medicinal herbs it describes were said to have been compiled more than 2,000 years earlier by the fabled 'Divine Farmer' Shennong. Legend has it that the mythological emperor, considered the father of Chinese medicine, dedicated himself to understanding the nature of medicinal herbs so much that he ingested dozens of plants each day and recorded their effects. He is credited with discovering the medicinal properties of cannabis during his lifespan, but it's hard to determine exactly when people started to drink the plant as a tea. The practice seems to have lingered in China over the centuries, but available evidence doesn't indicate the extent of such use until the late nineteenth century.

By then, references to *ma cha*, which the Chinese prepared by grinding up cannabis leaves and flowers to brew in a teapot with water, had increased. Depending on the region, various spices or herbs were added before it was strained and served hot. We don't know how often countercultural travellers encountered these drinks during the second half of the twentieth century, but *High Times* provided several references during its early years. However, smoking and eating cannabis remained far more popular, which might be because cannabis is not soluble in water. Since the Chinese prepared this tea for medical purposes, however, the intensity of its effects would not have been as valuable for them as it was for the countercultural consumers who went east in search of the plant for that purpose.

This is not to say that cannabinoids do not become available when brewed in water, but rather that the levels are too insignificant for a consumer to feel any effects. The longer the cannabis is allowed to simmer in the water, the more cannabinoid content the tea will have, but the levels are extremely low even after 30 minutes. Some studies have shown high levels of THC-A in teas brewed with THC flower, which may be why the Chinese considered it medicinal. Jamaica also has a high

Cannabis tea.

Margarita cocktail made with cannabis-infused tincture.

number of cannabis tea consumers, with those who partake reporting that the beverage is a valuable prophylactic and remedy for alleviating colds and fevers. The Netherlands does as well, and the Dutch Office of Medicinal Cannabis has claimed that brewing the plant in a tea is the most suitable form of medical consumption.[13]

By the time the remedicalization movement gave way to the recreational revolution of the 2010s, new methods were introduced by manufacturers interested in building a more vibrant culture around drinking cannabis. Before then, ethanol was the primary solvent used to prepare psychoactive liquid forms of the plant. However, there are many parallels in the diversity of flavours and tastes between cannabis and wine, so mixologists started experimenting with creating eclectic spirits and liqueurs for connoisseurs. Methods for mixing transformed significantly with the development of new technologies such as nano-emulsification, which essentially breaks cannabinoids down into microscopic droplets that are evenly distributed in water with emulsifiers. It's a complicated process that requires high-tech equipment and a laboratory setting, but it has transformed the quality and variation of cannabinoid-rich cocktails since 2019.

Canada became an attractive country for beverage company start-ups after it legalized cannabis in 2018, but the sector has continued to grow on an international scale since 2014 or so. The market has been flooded with various types of teas, tonics, liquors and brews containing different parts of the plant. Several styles of cannabis beer – including hempseed beer – have hit the market, as well as coffees infused with THC or CBD (or both), and sparkling wines and energy drinks with detailed measurements of terpenes and cannabinoids in each bottle or can. Pre-packaged cannabis-infused herbal teas also abound, with several companies even producing a product referred to as canna-bucha – a play on words that references an ancient form of fermented tea (kombucha) that has been infused with cannabis or hemp.

Even before nano-emulsification techniques opened the floodgates for cannabis-infused drinks, however, the mixologist and cannabis enthusiast Warren Bobrow had mastered the art of making craft cocktails with different preparations of the plant. In *Cannabis Cocktails, Mocktails and Tonics* (2016), he describes himself as a 'Cocktail Whisperer' whose craft is more akin to something like a modern apothecary than a venture-capitalist. Toronto's *Globe and Mail* referred to his emerging field as one of 'medicated mixology'.[14] He has a passion for promoting wellness and getting people to pay closer attention to the ingredients they use in the taste-making process that cannabis lends itself to when mixed with the right botanicals. The book includes 75 recipes and highlights the importance of focusing on decarboxylation when it comes to preparing the plant for consumption, which is an essential process for reaching

Warren Bobrow's spiced cannabis-infused mulled cider, featured in *High Times* (November 2018).

consistency and maximizing the bioavailability of the healing properties in the cocktails.

Before people like Bobrow, the culture of infusing cannabis into drinks mostly focused on how to make the plant into a liquid, but he sees it as an art form that accentuates the flavours of each cultivar with careful consideration to details. His meticulous focus on taste, palate and the safe consumption of cannabis as a form of both healing and recreation is a powerful reflection of how the plant has come full circle in returning to its medicinal roots and reclaiming its place as a valuable therapeutic agent in modern medicine.

EAT · IT!

by J. F. Burke

In the Americas we don't think of eating grass except on special occasions in brownies. But in North Africa, the Middle East and South Asia hundreds of millions of Hindus and Moslems eat grass as an item of diet. They call it bhang or ganja. They chew it, fresh or dried, and prepare it uncooked in candies and in a milk drink. And they've been doing this for hundreds of generations.

Cannabis was an important item in the *materia medica* of the ancient world. Specimens have been found in Egyptian archaeological sites nearly 4,000 years old. The ancient Thebans used it in a beverage. The Scythians grew hemp along the banks of the Volga 3,000 years ago. Chinese tradition puts the use of cannabis as early as 2000 B.C. Indian medical writing reports uses of cannabis before 1000 B.C.

The Greek physician Galen wrote in 160 A.D. that hemp in pastries produces

Eating marijuana and hashish is not only enjoyable, it's good for you

CAROL BOUMA

'Eat It!' by J. F. Burke, in *High Times* (February 1978), featuring artwork by Carol Bouman, 1977.

6
Cooking with Cannabis

Tell me what you eat, I'll tell you who you are.
Jean Anthelme Brillat-Savarin, *The Physiology of Taste* (1825)

Cooking is a way of life. It's deeply rooted in human history as one of the oldest forms of cultural expression. While the need to eat is universal, the way people go about doing it differs drastically from region to region. Methods of preparing a meal and selecting ingredients and the techniques and tools used to manipulate food all reflect the unique cultural identity that societies develop over time. This means cooking is something far more complex than a simple act of achieving sustenance. Instead, it's more like an intricate cultural process that involves tapping into a storehouse of knowledge to combine edible ingredients and transform them through the application of heat. The result is an artful creation that transcends the sum of its parts, making cooking a form of coded behaviour that invests meaning into the food we eat.

Not only does the culinary culture of a people differ from region to region, but the meaning of cooking within these regions also changes over time. In ancient and medieval history, for example, people had a far deeper connection with cooking and medicine than the fast-food cultures of the twenty-first century allow. Back then, cooking and medicine were so intertwined that eating served as a form of medication, whereas during the Enlightenment the impulse to extract medicinal plant properties bifurcated medicine from cooking. As the transatlantic slave trade gave way to an exponential growth in sugar production, cooking became more associated with taste and pleasure – eventually changing so drastically that people now must take medicine because of the food they eat. In fact, these days, more people die each year owing to dietary illnesses than they do from violence. Diabetes, heart disease and hypertension from our diets are more likely to harm us than a terrorist attack or an enemy invasion.

So, too, does the meaning of the ingredients we cook with change over time. What some generations used for one purpose can serve a much different function for others. Sugar has transformed in meaning multiple times since the Middle Ages, as has the chocolate that people consider so intricately tied to it in many cultural settings today. For Europeans, the tomato started out as an ornamental plant of suspicious character after they encountered it in the Americas, only for it to become a staple crop throughout the continent in the centuries that followed. Clearly, the way cultures form meaning out of their culinary practices has a lot to do with aspects of life that go beyond the digestive tract.

Cannabis is no exception. Eating majoun in Persia or Morocco during the nineteenth century did not carry the same cultural baggage as it did for mesmerists and spiritualists who consumed it to reach clairvoyance – even if they were inspired by its use in the so-called Orient. Preparing bhang as a group in Mughal India expressed entirely different coded behaviour than the ceremonial consumption practices of Club des Hashischins in nineteenth-century France. What it meant to eat a space cake in one of Amsterdam's early coffee shops was much removed from the meaning of eating Mary Rathbun's

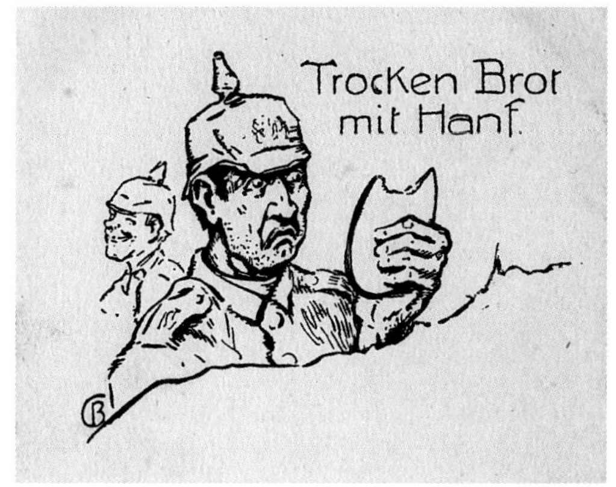

Trocken Brot mit Hanf, postcard, n.d. The translation is dry bread with hemp, which could be a joke pertaining to the taste of military food.

brownies in San Francisco in the 1980s, and both were drastically different from the purpose behind consuming a full-course meal consisting entirely of cannabis-infused cuisine at one of Los Angeles's Cannabis Supper Club events that have been taking place twice a month since 2017.

These are just a few examples that illustrate the cultural shifts in meaning behind preparing and consuming cannabis foods, not to mention all the non-psychoactive recipes like those found in *The Hemp Cookbook* (1998) or *The High Art of Cannabis Cuisine* (2020). Cooking with cannabis has become a lofty craft of savoury tastes and fancy flavours today, but this hasn't always been the case. As we saw with hempseed, people across many cultures have expressed a cultural disregard for eating the plant. Théophile Gautier described the taste of Jacques-Joseph Moreau's 'green paste' from the hashish club meetings as 'acrid', which Aleister Crowley used in his autobiography to describe the taste as well, only he added 'nauseous'. With some notable exceptions found in eastern Europe, Eurasia, some parts of the Caribbean and Southeast Asian countries such as Cambodia and Thailand, cannabis as an ingestible ingredient just wasn't that appealing.[1]

Even during the early days of the canna-brownie, in fact, the baked goods contained a peculiar texture that Alia Volz discussed in her memoir *Home Baked* (2020). Her mother, Meridy Volz, distributed thousands of the brownies in San Francisco during the 1970s and '80s through a clandestine operation called Sticky Fingers Brownies. The texture of ground-up cannabis as an ingredient left much to be desired, but the purpose behind consuming them wasn't about palate. The film *I Love You, Alice B. Toklas* alluded to this when some of the characters detected an unfamiliar texture in the cannabis brownies they ate. The appeal came from the after-effects – especially if they were cooked at lower temperatures, which Volz's mother discovered one day after her friend Barb forgot to add the flour and undercooked a batch that was gooey in the middle but more potent. As Volz pointed out, the 'absence of flour allowed the body to process [the cannabinoids] much faster', and the low heat helped 'release the THC without beginning to kill it off'.[2]

Another purpose behind people consuming baked cannabis goods so enthusiastically during the countercultural era, despite their taste, had to do with the inspirational form of Orientalism that attracted Westerners to the East, where edible preparations were more prevalent. Even the fudge that Brion Gysin contributed to Toklas's cookbook was inspired by cannabis cultures in Morocco, where he lived when he sent her the recipe. The year her book came out, in fact, he opened a restaurant in Tangier with his Moroccan friend Mohamed Hamri. They even called it 'The 1001 Nights'. The business didn't last long, and no evidence has yet to surface on what they served, but both were known for eating majoun in Morocco during the 1950s and '60s. Gysin also entertained a variety of visitors from several countries during his time as an expatriate there, which likely inspired some to cook with cannabis after returning home.

One of those visitors, in fact, was Ira Cohen, who visited Tangier in the early 1960s. By 1966 he was dating a woman named Rosalind who helped him publish 10,000 copies of a small booklet called *The Hashish Cookbook*. Subsequent editions came out in 1967, '74 and '99. Most of the 23 recipes included in the book reflect the influence of Indian, Moroccan and Middle Eastern traditions, but some, like the 'Christmas Pudding' and 'Seed Fritters', seem to have been original creations. Not much understanding of the science behind cooking with cannabis is presented, and in fact, some recipes, such as a tea that calls for

'Eat it, Baby!' logo created by Doug Volz for Sticky Fingers Brownies, 1977.

'The Age of Kali' packaging designed by Doug Volz for Sticky Fingers Brownies, 1979.

boiling parts of the plant in water, can't be very potent. Nevertheless, the pamphlet reflects the growing transatlantic trend towards what the late cannabis scholar Lester Grinspoon described as 'bringing marihuana out of the joint or pipe and into the kitchen'.[3] Part of that process was connected to the allure of Eastern cultures for those involved in the countercultural movement.

A more detailed book from 1967 contains many of the same recipes, but also 'Spaghetti'. It, too, leaves much to be desired when it comes to cooking with cannabis, but the author did provide insight into where the inspiration for doing so derived from: 'Marihuana is seldom . . . eaten in the forms described . . . [but] tourists frequently eat and drink these preparations when visiting [the Eastern] section of the world.'[4] In a similar cookbook published a few years later, the authors reiterated this point by proclaiming that it 'is to the gourmets of the West that this guide is addressed, for those of the East know the subject well enough to correct me on too many points'.[5] *Leaves of Grass* is another example, which includes recipes with orientalized names such as 'BHANG POPS', HASSANBURGERS' and 'MEAT BALLS ALI PASHA'.[6] Evelyn Schmevelyn's *Cooking with Marijuana* (1974) and George Vye and Stewart Grossman's *Cooking with Grass* (1976) reflect this inspirational form of Orientalism as well.

In Jamaica Afro-Caribbeans adopted the use of cannabis after Hindu and Muslim indentured servants from British India brought the plant there in the nineteenth century. By the 1960s it had become tightly integrated into the medicinal, spiritual and restorative drug cultures among some of the island's African diaspora population, for which Bob Marley became a transnational cultural icon. He used cannabis extensively, as did a higher proportion of Jamaicans compared to most cultures, where around 1 per cent of the population identifies with the Rastafarian religion that sanctions its consumption as a spiritual herb. Eating and drinking it was more prevalent there as well, but its primary association was still connected to smoking. Vera Rubin only used the verb 'to cook' twice in her book *Ganja in Jamaica* (1975), and she claimed to have only found 'occasional references . . . made in the community to the use of ganja in food'.[7] Teas and tonics appeared a bit more often, but cooking

Bob Marley in Kingston, *c.* 1974.

Jamaican ganja brownie store, 2017.

references were limited to a few dishes that included greens, gourds, bananas and some soups.

The countercultural cravings of cannabis tourists, on the other hand, brought edible enthusiasts to the island nation in search of new forms of consumption. While the plant remained illegal in Jamaica after independence (1962), a vibrant cannabis culture nevertheless persisted. Reports from travellers such as Chris Kilham, who visited Negril in the 1980s, described discreet storefronts like Miss Brown's Fine Foods that sold potent baked goods for decades with no attempt to mask the disagreeable texture of the ground-up cannabis within them. Fast forward to 2018, however – when the plant finally became legal in the country – and much tastier infusions such as muffins, smoothies and gourmet chocolates were available. Catering services with specialized chefs serving cannabis meals to enhance the dining experience replaced 'acrid' baked goods made purely for the purpose of getting high.

Something similar occurred in areas of the United States where consumption became legal at the state level. Regions across Canada, France, the Netherlands and the UK experienced seismic shifts in the cannabis dining experience also, as well as a growing number of European and African countries. The plant has expanded beyond the realm of marginalized identities and countercultural consumers, reaching into elements of high society that are, once again, adding new dimensions to the plant's cultural palette.

Bong Appétit

In 1978, just as the trend for cooking cannabis started gaining more traction, an article appeared in *High Times* titled 'Eat It!' The author, J. F. Burke, acknowledged that the concept hadn't taken off in the Americas yet, but that 'hundreds of millions of Hindus and Moslems eat grass as an item of diet'. Burke also discussed 'an Arabian Nights experience that lasted three days' after eating some hashish candy, but the article presented cannabis as a healthy food option that could be eaten raw or cooked. Soups, stew, cereal, salad, pastries, brownies and majoun were mentioned too, but there wasn't much on how to unlock the plant's potential as a cooking agent. Instead, the general practice of tossing some ground-up plant material into a recipe is about as far as Burke went. He did, however, provide important insight into one aspect of how to improve the cooking process by mentioning that the plant's psychoactive properties are not 'water-soluble and won't dissolve in most preparations'.[8]

The need for a keener understanding of cannabis chemistry became more apparent as more people joined in the cooking craze. Infusions such as soaking the inflorescences in olive oil at room temperature for a few weeks or sautéing cannabis in butter are not that difficult to prepare, and extracting cannabinoids with solvents had a long history by then. Nevertheless, these methods limited cooking options to the use of lipids and alcohol. Nano-emulsification eliminated this issue, and the creation of concentrated, water-soluble cannabis powders and liquids significantly reshaped the cooking process. Methods such as *sous vide* cooking (low-temperature, long-time cooking) and the isolation of terpene concentrates to enhance flavour capacities, elevate the senses and improve dish pairings also brought significant advancements. All this, combined with more awareness of the roles that decarboxylation and heat play in activating cannabinoids – as well as the taste value that comes from leaching the plant ingredient in water overnight before using it – significantly improved the consumer experience behind eating cooked cannabis.

By the 2010s a cannabis cooking revolution was under way. Amsterdam's famous Cannabis Cup expanded into more cities, and use of the plant stretched far beyond the underground

Canna-butter.

economies of the countercultural era. Cannabis dining clubs and elegant social gatherings such as LA's Cannabis Supper Club started surfacing, with specialized chefs who experimented with all sorts of culinary combinations in the hopes of exciting the palates of those interested in exploring the plant's culinary potential. Cookbooks and cannabis guides continued flooding the market, and *High Times* expanded its culinary boundaries by introducing a popular column titled 'Psychedelic Kitchen'. The march towards legitimacy and cultural acceptability is by no means complete or even fully secured today, but the expansion of cannabis consumption into these broader dimensions of high society has tipped the scale in favour of it eventually becoming so.

The opulence that came with these developments, however, stands in stark contrast to the privation that still exists for racial minorities, those struggling with PTSD or other mental-health illnesses and economically disadvantaged people whose lives have been derailed by their consumption practices. In 2016, for example, thousands of people were still being arrested across the United States for merely possessing a preparation of the plant, yet the production company Viceland debuted a reality television series called *Bong Appétit* that depicted extravagant cannabis dinner parties taking place in the same country. The show aired for three seasons and contained dozens of episodes portraying carefree consumers enjoying the fine-dining experience of full-course meals at a home in Los Angeles, where everything they ate was infused with some part of the plant. Each episode began with the host showing off their massive cupboard full of enough cannabis products to send someone to prison for decades just a few states over in places like Idaho, Kansas, Nebraska and Wyoming.

A cookbook based off the show came out in 2018, in which the authors addressed this contrast by pointing out – rather bluntly – how 'it's incredibly fucked up that there are millions of people in prison for enjoying the kind of recreational activity you're about to read an entire book on.' They also wanted their audience to 'please know we're sorry – and . . . we're hoping that changes soon.' In the meantime, however, the proverbial show must go on, and indeed it did; quite literally in the real show, in fact, which the book described as a 'cutting-edge' cannabis television series that 'redefines luxury in many respects'.[9] The combinations of terpenes and cannabinoids that the chefs experimented with reflects something similar to what Michael Pollan defined over two decades earlier as the rise of a 'connoisseurship of cannabis – not just of its taste or aroma, but of the specific psychological texture of its high'.[10] He wrote that comment in reference to the sea change in quality that cannabis endured back in the 1990s, but it just as easily applies to the cultural scene of cooking with the plant today.

Of course, where there's connoisseurship, commercialization often follows. Cannabis has been notoriously difficult to commercialize because of its botanical diversity and oscillating legal status, but entrepreneurially driven venture capitalists have been making strides. Some would call them setbacks, however, for they see commercialization as a distraction from the plant's natural medicine, exploiting vulnerable people for profit, prioritizing quantity over quality and compromising the ability of craft cultivators to grow an extremely versatile, multifaceted and highly useful plant on their own.

Holistic Healing

The concept of commercializing cannabis has caused considerable concern among advocates whose perceptions of the plant do not align with the culture of mass consumerism that threatens to pervade the industry. From their perspective, commercialization represents a departure from the plant's history as an agent of healing and dilutes the authentic cultural significance that has been associated with cannabis for centuries. Instead, they emphasize the importance of recognizing and preserving the plant's natural therapeutic properties and maintaining a holistic approach to its use. They also call for a more mindful approach to integrating the plant into the economy – one that respects the origins of its historical roots, allows those with extensive knowledge of the plant who were criminalized for non-violent violations to gain a seat at the table and acknowledges its potential to promote the physical, spiritual and emotional well-being of humanity.

For these critics, the true essence of cannabis lies in its ability to foster holistic healing. Nico Murillo, for example, is the founder and CEO of a LLC called Bocanna that provides educational opportunities, and seeks to cultivate, process and

Nico Murillo with her hemp plants, 2023.

distribute low-level THC products to patients who are enrolled in the Texas Compassionate Use Program (TCUP). She also serves on the board of directors for a non-profit organization called Texans for Safe Access, which supports the right of all Texans to safe and legal access to cannabis for therapeutic use and research. Texas is still one of the most restrictive U.S. states when it comes to cannabis, but in 2015, legislation passed that allows TCUP to provide patients with access to CBD and low-level THC cannabis-infused oils and edibles. In 2019 Murillo and her team helped lobby for another bill to get the state to increase the maximum THC level, but the percentage is still among the lowest in the nation.

Murillo became a staunch advocate for access to cannabis as medicine after she 'started seeing moms whose kids were hurting and this woman had a non-verbal daughter with autism whose quality of life drastically improved after consuming cannabis'. As a certified chef with years of experience in the food industry, she is keenly aware of the historical connection between food and medicine: 'Plants have always been medicinal. If you go back to the basics then you find the key to wellness, which is eating natural foods from scratch, not processed foods or cheap food grown in the field with all sorts of chemicals.' By preparing food with cannabis, she argues, we 'increase access to wellness because cannabis is medicine. This is a global movement of healing and of trying to find balance through spiritual awakening, through medicine, and through returning to a more natural diet.' Commercialization, however, stifles this movement by 'causing cannabis to become a processed item, which eliminates the valuable entourage effect of whole plant medicine that many believe makes up the cannabis plant'.[11]

Historically speaking, commercialization has often compromised the integrity of medicinal plants. Tobacco is a case in point, as well as ginseng root, Palo Santo wood and ayahuasca.

Earth Medicine poster, 2011.

These are just a few examples that reflect the drastic transformations that traditional plant medicines go through when societies prioritize profits and mass production over small-scale craft cultivation, yield maximization and product standardization over quality and variability, and synthetic medicines over holistic healing. Corporate entities could buy up patents, companies and brands to control the supply and variation of available cannabis. Big Pharma and large-scale agricultural conglomerates such as the one that Canopy Growth Corporation is now building in Canada have also furrowed the brows of those who worry about the effects cannabis commercialization will have on the plant.

Marginalizing the type of craft cultivation that was developed by those who formed a deep understanding of the plant's versatility and genetic diversity is also concerning for advocates of holistic healing. As large corporations enter the market to dominate the industry, smaller or lesser-known producers get left behind, leading to a loss of cultural heritage and traditional knowledge associated with the plant. Africans preserved unique cannabis strains by saving seeds from landrace cultivars such as Durban Poison for centuries, yet they rarely get credit or even acknowledgement for doing so.[12] Unfortunately, in fact, the legacy of European colonialism has left Africa as one of the most restrictive continents in the world when it comes to cannabis laws, where it remains illegal everywhere except (for medical use only) in Lesotho (2017), Zimbabwe (2018) and Malawi (2020).

Corporate cannabis still seems quite a way away however, if it is even possible. Arguments such as those put forth by Ryan Stoa in his book *Craft Weed: Family Farming and the Future of the Marijuana Industry* (2018) stress how difficult cannabis is to mass produce, and we have not seen any of these developments in South American countries such as Uruguay, Peru, Chile,

Ecuador, Colombia and Argentina – where the plant has been either legal or decriminalized since the late twentieth century. However, that could all change if the United States federally legalizes it, and it's still too early to tell how things will turn out in Canada's legal market. But for those who see the plant as a healing agent with the capacity to restore humanity's relationship between food and medicine that it lost during the industrial revolution, commercialization is a grim prospect.

Recipes

Most of these recipes specify amounts of cannabis to add as an ingredient, but quality and potency varies significantly. Try to find the cannabinoid profile of a batch of cannabis before using it and consult a cannabis professional if you are unfamiliar with the plant. Tolerance is also important to consider, for overconsumption of THC can cause extreme paranoia and/or psychological discomfort for a few hours before subsiding. Always start out with smaller dosages and work your way up. Remember that it can take up to two hours for some people to feel the effects of eating cannabis in some circumstances, so be careful. Any of the recipes can replace CBD for THC, or vice versa, but the modern ones that refer to hemp are non-psychoactive. Also remember that the key to cannabis gastronomy lies in how the plant is prepared before the cooking process begins, so it is important to understand decarboxylation, heat application and the binding of cannabinoids to lipids before you start.

Historic Recipes

Medical Cannabis Extract

William Brooke O'Shaughnessy, *On the Preparations of the Indian Hemp . . .* (1839)

The *resinous extract* is prepared by boiling the rich, adhesive tops of the dried Gunjah in spirits until all resin is dissolved. The tincture thus obtained is evaporated to dryness in a vessel placed over a pot of boiling water. The extract softens at a gentle heat and can be made into pills without any addition.

The *tincture* is prepared by dissolving three grains of the extract in one drachm of proof spirit.

Madjoum

L. Raynaud, *Étude sur l'hygiène et la médecine au Maroc . . .* (1902)

The leaves and seeds are boiled in very little water; then, oil or butter is added. The whole mixture should cook for another two hours and be left to cool. The water and debris of the plant settles at the bottom of the container, while the oily or fatty extract floats to the top. It is this extract that is used [to cook with], either pure or mixed with almonds, nuts or honey.

The usual dose is one *gros pois* [large pea-sized amount], but regular users easily consume up to four or five *boulettes* [small balls] to achieve the intoxicating effect. They also simultaneously consume tea, which is said to help accelerate the euphoria.

Alice B. Toklas Haschich Fudge

Brion Gysin, 1954

Take 1 teaspoon black peppercorns, 1 whole nutmeg, 4 average sticks of cinnamon, 1 teaspoon coriander. These should all be pulverized in a mortar. About a handful each of stoned dates, dried figs, shelled almonds and peanuts; chop these and mix them together. A bunch of canibus sativa can be pulverized. This along with the spices should be dusted over the mixed fruit and nuts, kneaded together. About a cup of sugar dissolved in a big pot of butter. Rolled into a cake and cut into pieces or made into balls about the size of a walnut, it should be eaten with care. Two pieces are quite sufficient.

Haschich

Réne Brunel, *Le Monachisme errant dans l'Islam* (1955)

The tops and the widest leaves of hemp are collected and dried in the sun, then roasted in a pan. Afterward, they are rolled and transformed into fine powder. This powder is then mixed with roasted sorghum or barley and pounded in the proportion of ⅓ hemp and ⅔ sorghum or barley flour . . . To make the mixture less bitter in taste, powdered salt is added.

Sticky Fingers Brownies

Barbara Hartman-Jenichen [1976], first published in Alia Volz, *Home Baked: My Mom, Marijuana, and the Stoning of San Francisco* (2020)

8 oz (225 g) magic (oven-dried, powdered in a food processor, sifted, California-grown sin semilla leaf [seedless cannabis])
Note: Chaff [hashish or kiff] may be used later for grass oil
5 sticks butter
16 eggs
6 cups (1¼ kg) sugar
3 cups (360 g) flour
3 tbsp baking powder
¼ tsp salt
16 oz unsweetened baking chocolate

Melt butter in a double boiler and stir in the magic. This is the 'ghee'. Combine eggs and sugar in a large bowl. Slowly melt chocolate in another double boiler. When the ghee has cooked for 30 minutes, add flour, powder, salt to eggs and sugar. Then add the ghee and the chocolate. Pour into four 9" × 12" greased baking pans. Bake at 205°C/ 400°F, patting down the batter several times with a spatula to keep it from rising. When the brownies are solid, but still very moist, remove from oven and cover with a towel to keep moisture in. Yields eight dozen 2" × 2" brownies. Power to the People. We love you. Sticky Fingers Brownies.

Modern Recipes

Cannabis Butter

450 g (2 cups) of butter
30 g (1 oz) quality cannabis trim
or
10 g high-quality cannabis flower

Puree the cannabis in a blender with water and use a cheese cloth to strain. Repeat three times, then wring the plant material out with the cheese cloth.

Preheat oven to 125°C/255°F and spread the clean, blended cannabis out to decarboxylate in the oven for 25 minutes.

Sauté cannabis in butter over medium heat for 30 minutes. Spread it out evenly so that all the plant material remains submerged in the butter. Stir occasionally.

Strain butter through a cheese cloth, wringing the mixture out of the plant material and into a container with a lid.

Store butter in refrigerator for three weeks to use in recipes, on toast or in oatmeal.

Gluten-Free Chocolate Canna-Banana Bread

Tracee Tovanché

(*For 3 loaves*)
250 g (2 cups) almond flour
40 g (⅓ cup) unsweetened cocoa powder
1 tsp bicarbonate of soda
½ tsp sea salt
115 g/120 ml (4 oz) canna-butter, softened
170 g/120 ml (6 oz) honey
3 large eggs
1 tsp apple cider vinegar
1 tsp vanilla extract
250 ml (1 cup) mashed very ripe banana
250 g (9 oz) chopped walnuts

Preheat oven to 165°C/330°F. Cut three pieces of parchment paper to 12.5 × 25 cm (5 in. × 10 in.). Grease pans and lay parchment covering the long edge, allowing it to hang over each side to make a hammock. Place lined pans on a large baking sheet.

Whisk almond flour, cocoa powder, bicarbonate of soda and sea salt in a medium-sized mixing bowl until combined.

Whisk the canna-butter and honey in large mixing bowl until smooth and creamy. Whisk in eggs until blended, then add the apple cider vinegar and vanilla.

Stir in dry mixture just until combined, then stir in bananas until blended. Add the walnuts.

Pour batter into prepared pans. Place the baking sheet in the oven. Bake for 35 to 45 minutes, until loaves test clean with a toothpick. Do not overbake.

Run a butter knife down the short sides of each loaf. Use the parchment paper handles to remove each loaf. Let cool completely on a wire rack. Wrap each cooled loaf in a paper towel and then place in a sealed plastic bag or container and refrigerate. Keeps for one week. To freeze, wrap each loaf in waxed paper and place in a sealed plastic bag or freezer container to keep for three months.

Brisadeiros

Joshua Birchall

(A play on the traditional Brazilian dessert Brigadeiro, but with some extra 'breeze' in it)

110 g (4 oz) cannabis-infused butter
415 ml (14 oz) sweetened condensed milk
2 tbsp pure cacao

Add condensed milk, canna-butter and two tablespoons of pure cocoa to a saucepan over medium heat. Stir with spatula and turn down to medium-low once it starts to boil. Keep stirring for about 10 minutes until the mixture starts to thicken. Be sure to scrape the bottom and sides constantly so it doesn't burn.

Spread the mixture on a plate or glass casserole dish to cool. It should stiffen up as it cools.

Traditionally, people butter their hands and roll the caramel-like fudge into little balls as it stiffens, adding candy sprinkles (hundreds and thousands), crushed nuts, cocoa nibs or shredded coconut in the process. They can be placed into little doily cups or eaten with a spoon.

Serves 4

Caprese with Hemp Pesto and Hemp-Infused Olive Oil

Nico Murillo

Caprese

3 medium heirloom (heritage) tomatoes
Buffalo mozzarella
hemp-infused olive oil
extra virgin olive oil

Hemp pesto

45 g (1½ oz) hemp seeds
2 tbsp minced garlic

450 g (2 cups, packed) fresh basil
2 tbsp lemon juice
3 tbsp nutritional yeast
115 g (4 oz) Parmesan cheese
¼ tsp Celtic sea salt
pinch of black pepper
170 g (6 fl. oz) extra virgin olive oil
2 tsp hemp-infused extra virgin olive oil

To make the pesto

Add all pesto ingredients into a food processor (except the regular olive oil, hemp-infused olive oil and the lemon juice) and process until semi-smooth. Add olive oil in a small stream until it is incorporated. Add the lemon juice and blend for a few seconds. Turn processor off and use or store it in the fridge until meal is ready.
Serves 2–4

To plate the Caprese

Clean tomatoes and allow them to come to room temperature. Slice tomatoes about 6 mm (⅕ in.) thick and place them on a plate. Season tomatoes with salt and pepper. Cut mozzarella cheese and place it on the tomatoes. Add dollops of the hemp pesto. Drizzle additional infused oil on the tomatoes and cheese. Enjoy immediately.

Modern Majoun

Tracee Tovanché

(20 pieces)
120 g (1 cup) raw almonds
120 g (1 cup) raw cashews
85 g (¼ cup) pitted dates
100 g (3½ oz) chopped dried figs
1½ tsp ground ginger
1½ tsp ground cinnamon
½ tsp sea salt
½ tsp ground coriander

¼ tsp ground turmeric
¼ tsp ground black pepper
¼ tsp ground cardamom
¼ tsp ground nutmeg
¼ tsp ground cloves
pinch of ground cayenne pepper
4 tbsp honey
3 tbsp canna-butter

Pulse nuts in a food processor until ground. Remove about 70 g (2½ oz) and put in a small bowl and set aside.

Add spices to remaining nuts and pulse just until blended. Add honey and canna-butter. Pulse until mixture forms into a sticky paste.

Roll mixture into 3 cm balls and roll in reserved ground nuts. Chill until firm. Taste improves the next day when spices have mingled.

Tomato and Peach Hempseed Salad

Nico Murillo

710 g (25 oz) baby bibb lettuce, cleaned and chopped
2 heirloom (heritage) tomatoes, sliced
1 yellow peach, pitted and sliced
1 tbsp hempseed
2 tbsp pumpkin seeds
3 tbsp almonds, chopped
4 tbsp goat cheese, crumbled
4 tbsp dried cranberries
3 tbsp hemp-infused balsamic vinaigrette

Hemp-infused balsamic vinaigrette
60 g (2 oz) balsamic vinegar
1 tbsp Dijon mustard
113 g (4 oz) maple syrup
1 g (⅙ tsp) salt
pinch of pepper

90 g (3 fl. oz) avocado oil
8 g (1 tsp) hemp-infused olive oil

Place balsamic vinegar, mustard, maple syrup, salt and pepper into a food processor/blender. Blend on high. Combine avocado oil and hemp-infused olive oil, slow and steady, until it's blended and homogenized.

Use immediately or store in the fridge until ready for use.

To assemble the salad

Place the bibb lettuce on a chilled salad plate. Add sliced tomatoes and peaches, then sprinkle in hemp seeds, pumpkin seeds, almonds and dried cranberries. Add the crumbled goat cheese and drizzle hemp-infused balsamic vinaigrette on top of the salad. Enjoy immediately.
Serves 2

Ribeye with Hemp-Infused Butter

Nico Murillo

rib-eye beef
unsalted butter, softened
hemp-infused butter
salt
pepper

Bring the steak to 20°C/70°F before cooking, coating both sides with softened butter. Season both sides of the steak with salt and pepper.

Get the pan hot but not smoking; cast iron is best.

Place the steak in pan and cook about 4 minutes per side. Use a thermometer to ensure preferred cooking temperature (57°C/135°F for medium-well). Let the steak rest for about 4 minutes before adding hemp-infused butter to the top. Slice and serve immediately.
Serves 1

Chai Spice Breakfast Cookies with Hemp Hearts

Tracee Tovanché

(24 cookies)

150 g (1 cup) gluten-free rolled oats
100 g (1 cup) almond flour
120 g (4 oz) hemp hearts
1 tsp ground cinnamon
1 tsp ground ginger
½ tsp sea salt
½ tsp bicarbonate of soda
½ tsp ground allspice
¼ tsp ground cardamom
¼ tsp ground black pepper
60 ml melted butter
125 ml (4 fl. oz) maple syrup or honey
1 large egg
75–150 g (⅔–¾ cup) raisins

Preheat oven to 160°C/320°F and line a large baking sheet with parchment paper.

Add oats, almond flour, hemp hearts, spices, sea salt and bicarbonate of soda to a large mixing bowl. Whisk until combined.

Pour melted butter and maple syrup or honey into a small mixing bowl. Whisk until creamy. When mixture has cooled to room temperature, whisk in the egg.

Pour butter mixture into flour mixture and stir just until blended, then stir in the raisins.

Roll the dough into walnut-sized balls with wet hands. Place them about 5 cm (2 in.) apart on lined baking sheet.

Bake for 17 to 19 minutes, turning the pan halfway through baking time.

White Margarita Chicken Pizza with Hemp-Infused Olive Oil

Nico Murillo

any pizza dough recipe
180 g (1 cup) mozzarella
2 medium heirloom (heritage) tomatoes
1 bunch fresh basil, torn or chopped
1 tsp hemp-infused olive oil
3 tbsp extra virgin olive oil
1 container burrata cheese
180 g (5 oz) cooked cubed chicken

Alfredo sauce

180 g (6 oz) double (heavy) cream
280 g (10 oz) Parmesan cheese
¼ medium onion, chopped
pinch of Celtic sea salt
pinch of black or white pepper

Bring the heavy cream and onion to a low simmer. Add the Parmesan cheese and cook for 8 minutes or until it thickens slightly. Remove from heat and allow it to cool, then puree the mixture in a blender until smooth. Transfer to a clean pot, then add salt and pepper. Cook until it is thickened to a good sauce consistency, or it coats the back of a spoon. Allow the mixture to cool before adding to pizza base.

To prepare the pizza

Follow the pizza dough recipe directions for baking. Place the sauce on the pizza base, leaving 2.5 cm (1 in.) gap from the sides. Top with mozzarella and chicken. Cook until cheese is bubbly, then place the sliced tomatoes on the hot pizza. Add the burrata cheese and fresh basil. Combine regular olive oil and the hemp-infused olive oil. Drizzle with the oil on the pizza evenly. Enjoy warm!

Serves 2–4

Bhang Thandai

Tracee Tovanché

(1 litre serving)

45 g (¼ cup) whole raw almonds

1 tbsp shelled pistachios

1 tbsp raw cashews

3 green cardamom pods (or ½ tsp ground)

1 tsp fennel seed

10 peppercorns

¼ tsp ground turmeric

¾ tsp bhang powder or ground cannabis

dash of sea salt

1 litre (1 quart) whole milk (you can substitute half cream for some of the milk)

3 tbsp honey

1 tsp rosewater

To make the masala mixture, soak nuts and cardamom pods (if using) in a small bowl of water overnight, then drain. Alternatively, soak them in boiling water for an hour. Do not use roasted or salted nuts.

Add soaked nuts and pods to the bowl of a food processor, then add ground cardamom (if not using pods), fennel seeds, peppercorns, turmeric, cannabis and salt. Pulse just until paste is formed.

Heat milk in a saucepan until warm, then stir in the honey and masala. Bring to a low simmer, stirring occasionally, for about 10 minutes. Do not boil.

Remove from heat and stir in the rosewater. Cover and let steep for an hour, then strain through a fine mesh strainer to remove masala mixture.

Chill at least six hours before serving with ice and diluting with more milk if desired. Garnish with some ground nuts or rose petals.

References

1 What Is Cannabis?

1 Georges Métailié, 'Some Reflections on the History of Botanical Knowledge in China', *Circumscribere*, III (2007), pp. 66–84.
2 Robert C. Clarke and Mark D. Merlin, *Cannabis: Evolution and Ethnobotany* (Berkeley, CA, 2013), p. 207.
3 Benjamin Kemper, 'The Quest for an Ancient Culture's Cannabis-Filled Cooking', www.atlasobscura.com, 2 May 2018.
4 United Nations, *Single Convention on Narcotic Drugs* (New York, 1961), p. 1.
5 Susan Nance, *How the Arabian Nights Inspired the American Dream, 1790–1935* (Chapel Hill, NC, 2009).
6 For one example, see 'The Working Farmer', *A United States Journal* (1862), p. 282, available at www.google.com/books.
7 Anonymous, *England Illustrated; or, A Compendium of the Natural History, Geography, Topography, and Antiquities Ecclesiastical and Civil, of England and Wales. With Maps of the Several Counties, and Engravings of Many Remains of Antiquity, Remarkable Buildings, and Principal Towns*, vol. II (London, 1764), p. 21.
8 Hem Chunder Kerr, 'Report of the Cultivation of, and Trade in, Ganja in Bengal', 2 April 1877; Arthur Godley, ed., *Copies of the Following Papers Relating to the Consumption of Ganja and Other Drugs in India* (London, 1893), p. 107.

9 Jim Rendon, *Super-Charged: How Outlaws, Hippies, and Scientists Reinvented Marijuana* (Portland, OR, 2012).
10 *Physicians Drug News: A Journal of Pharmacy for Physicians*, X (1915), p. 62.
11 Nick Johnson, *Grass Roots: A History of Cannabis in the American West* (Corvallis, OR, 2017), p. 26.
12 'GROW YOUR OWN' advert, *High Times*, 1 November 1976, p. 103.
13 Danny Danko and T. H. Caeczar, 'The 65 Greatest Seed Banks of All Time', *High Times*, 1 March 2019, p. 65.

2 Cannabis Chemistry and Pharmacology

1 Peter Grinspoon, *Seeing through the Smoke: A Cannabis Specialist Untangles the Truth about Marijuana* (Essex, CT, 2023).
2 Ibid., p. 230.
3 For two examples, see Nishi Whiteley, *Chronic Relief: A Guide to Cannabis for the Terminally and Chronically Ill* (Austin, TX, 2016) and Julie Holland, ed., *The Pot Book: A Complete Guide to Cannabis: Its Role in Medicine, Politics, Science, and Culture* (Rochester, VT, 2010).
4 Isaac Campos, *Home Grown: Marijuana and the Origins of Mexico's War on Drugs* (Chapel Hill, NC, 2012), p. 8.
5 Richard DeGrandpre, *The Cult of Pharmacology: How America Became the World's Most Troubled Drug Culture* (Durham, NC, 2006), pp. viii, 27.
6 Chris Duvall, *Cannabis* (London, 2015), pp. 153–9.
7 Campos, *Home Grown*, p. 7; James H. Mills, *Cannabis Britannica: Empire, Trade, and Prohibition* (Oxford, 2003), p. 93.
8 DeGrandpre, *Cult of Pharmacology*, p. 120.
9 Kyle Jaeger, 'Scientists Published More Than 32,000 Marijuana Studies over the Past 10 Years, Including Thousands in 2023, NORML Analysis Says', www.marijuanamoment.net, 25 December 2023.

3 Hempseed in World History

1 Fabian Braitsch, 'Buddha Diet: Eat Only Hemp Seeds for Weeks', https://hempions.com, accessed 26 July 2023.
2 Chris S. Duvall, *The African Roots of Marijuana* (London, 2019).
3 John Hill, *A History of the Materia Medica . . .* (London, 1751), p. 535.
4 Nicholas Culpepper, *The English Physician Enlarged; with Three Hundred and Sixty-Nine Medicines, Made of English Herbs* (London, 1714), pp. 165–6.
5 Bradley J. Borougerdi, *Commodifying Cannabis: A Cultural History of a Complex Plant in the Atlantic World* (Lanham, MD, 2018), p. 26.
6 John Worlidge, *A Compleat System of Husbandry and Gardening* (London, 1716), p. 271; J. C. Hervieux de Chanteloup, *A New Treatise of Canary-Birds . . .* (London, 1718), p. 37.
7 Henry Livingston, *The Money Maker: Or How to Get Rich* (New York, 1868), p. 61; Edward Ward, *The Secret History of Clubs* (London, 1709), p. 177.
8 Duvall, *African Roots of Marijuana*, p. 143.
9 Isaac Campos, *Home Grown: Marijuana and the Origins of Mexico's War on Drugs* (Chapel Hill, NC, 2012), pp. 56–62.
10 For more details, see Borougerdi, *Commodifying Cannabis*, pp. 44–57.
11 James H. Mills, *Cannabis Nation: Control and Consumption in Britain, 1928–2008* (Oxford, 2013), pp. 17–22.
12 Letter from Joseph. B. Hertzfeld to the U.S. Department of Agriculture, 2 October 1935, File 0480-36: 'Marihuana (District #3)', Records of the Drug Enforcement Administration, Record Group 170, Box 110A, National Archives and Records Administration at College Park, MD.
13 Raymond Evans, U.S. Department of Agriculture, 'Hemp For Victory' (1942), available at https://archive.org; quotes appear in the film between the 2:09 to 2:52 minute mark.

14 Malcolm Mackinnon, 'Desert Showdown', *High Times*, 1 April 1995, p. 48.
15 Jack Herer, 'Can Pot Save the World?' *High Times*, 1 February 1989, p. 36.
16 Don Wirtshafter, 'Why Hemp Seeds?', in *Hemp Today*, ed. Ed Rosenthal (Oakland, CA, 1994), p. 169.
17 Ralf Hiener, Bettina Mack, Matthias Schillo and Stefan Wirner, *The Hemp Cookbook* (Berkeley, CA, 1999), p. 10.
18 Todd Dalotto, *The Hemp Cookbook: From Seed to Shining Seed* (Rochester, VT, 2000), p. 3.
19 Wirtshafter, 'Why Hemp Seeds?', p. 169.

4 Eating Cannabis

1 Jessica Caporuscio, 'Eating Raw Weed: Can It Get You High?', *Medical News Today*, www.medicalnewstoday.com, 25 February 2022.
2 Robert C. Clarke and Mark D. Merlin, *Cannabis: Evolution and Ethnobotany* (Berkeley, CA, 2013), pp. 1–6.
3 Mark D. Merlin, *Man and Marijuana: Some Aspects of Their Ancient Relationship* (Rutherford, NJ, 1972), pp. 40–45.
4 Robyn Griggs Lawrence, *Pot in Pans: A History of Eating Cannabis* (Lanham, MD, 2019), p. 25.
5 Shafique N. Virani, 'An Old Man, a Garden, and an Assembly of Assassins: Legends and Realities of the Nizari Ismaili Muslims', *Iran*, LXI/2 (2021), p. 274; M. Silvestre de Sacy, 'Mémoire: Sur la dynastie des Assassins et sur l'origine de leur nom', *Séance publique d'Institut*, 7 July 1809, available at www.google.com/books.
6 David A. Guba Jr, *Taming Cannabis: Drugs and Empire in Nineteenth-Century France* (London, 2020), p. 89.
7 William Brooke O'Shaughnessy, *On the Preparations of the Indian Hemp or Gunjah (Cannabis Indica), Their Effects on the Animal System in Health, and Their Utility in the Treatment of Tetanus and Other Convulsive Disorders* (Calcutta, 1839), p. 1, located in the Indian Office Records at the British Library

Asian and African Reading Room, Tracts 25 (f); excerpts can also be found in The Acting Secretaries, eds, *Journal of the Asiatic Society of Bengal*, III (1840), pp. 735–6, available online at https://archive.org.

8 Guba, *Taming Cannabis*, p. 99.

9 Théophile Gautier, 'Le Club des Hachichins', *Revue de deux mondes* (February 1846), pp. 320, 325, quoted in Guba, *Taming Cannabis*, p. 155.

10 Fitz Hugh Ludlow, *The Hasheesh Eater: Being Passages from the Life of a Pythagorean* (New York, 1857), p. 18.

11 Ibid., pp. 18–19.

12 Anonymous, 'Literary Notices', *Harper's New Monthly Magazine*, XV/90 (1857), pp. 834–5; Anonymous, 'Hasheesh', *Saturday Review*, V/120 (1858), pp. 166–7; Anonymous, 'Narcotics', *North American Review*, XCV/197 (1862), p. 375.

13 Paschal Beverly Randolph, *The Guide to Clairvoyance, and Clairvoyant's Guide: A Practical Manual for Those Who Aim at Perfect Clear Seeing and Psychometry; Also, A Special Paper Concerning Hashish, Its Uses, Abuses, and Dangers, Its Extasia, Fantasia, and Illuminati* (Boston, MA, 1867), p. 14.

14 Ibid., pp. 32–9.

15 John Patrick Deveney, *Paschal Beverly Randolph: A Nineteenth-Century Black American Spiritualist, Rosicrucian, and Sex Magician* (Albany, NY, 1997), p. 417.

16 Paschal Beverly Randolph, *The Rosicrucian Dream Book* (Boston, MA, 1871), p. 58.

17 Christopher Partridge, *High Culture: Drugs, Mysticism, and the Pursuit of Transcendence in the Modern World* (New York, 2018), p. 166; Walter Benjamin, *On Hashish*, trans. Howard Eiland et al. (London, 2006), p. viii.

18 Emily Temple, 'Here It Is: Alice B. Toklas's Recipe for Hash Brownies', https://lithub.com, 20 November 2018.

19 Emily Dufton, *Grass Roots: The Rise and Fall and Rise of Marijuana in America* (New York, 2017), p. 207.

5 Drinking Cannabis

1 Sophie Saint Thomas, 'Charlotte's Web: A CBD Origin Story', *High Times*, 2 December 2019, pp. 44–50.
2 'Marijuana Leaf Plays Epilepsy Cure Role', *Salt Lake City Telegram*, 20 May 1949, in Department of Justice, Bureau of Narcotics and Dangerous Drugs, Subject Files, 1916–1970, Record Group 170, Container 110, National Archives and Records Administration at College Park, MD.
3 Maziyar Ghiabi, 'The Pluriverse of Intoxication: Words, Lives, Worlds in Islamicate History', *Social History of Alcohol and Drugs*, XXXVI/2 (2022), pp. 140–41.
4 Utathya Chattopadhyaya, 'Reading Cannabis in the Colony: Law, Nomenclature, and Proverbial Knowledge in British India', *Social History of Alcohol and Drugs*, XXXVI/2 (2022), p. 201.
5 Joseph S. Alter, *The Wrestler's Body: Identity and Ideology in North India* (Berkeley, CA, 1992), p. 155.
6 James H. Mills, *Cannabis Britannica: Empire, Trade, and Prohibition* (Oxford, 2003), p. 29.
7 Samuel Hahnemann, *Materia Medica Pura* [1830], vol. I, trans. R. E. Dudgeon (London, 1880), p. 321.
8 William Brooke O'Shaughnessy, *On the Preparations of the Indian Hemp, or Gunjah (Cannabis Indica), Their Effects on the Animal System in Health, and Their Utility in the Treatment of Tetanus and Other Convulsive Diseases* (London, 1843), p. 35.
9 'Golden Age of Medical Cannabis', https://hashmuseum.com, accessed 1 August 2023.
10 Robert Edmund Scoresby-Jackson, *Note-Book of Materia Medica, Pharmacology and Therapeutics*, 2nd edn (Edinburgh and London, 1871), p. 547.
11 William Osler, *The Principles and Practice of Medicine* (Edinburgh and London, 1892), pp. 956, 959.
12 Mary Ought Six, 'Ride the Dragon', *High Times*, 1 November 2013, p. 34.
13 Arno Hazekamp et al., 'Cannabis Tea Revisited: A Systematic Evaluation of the Cannabinoid Composition of Cannabis Tea', *Journal of Ethnopharmacology*, CXIII/1 (2007), p. 90.

14 'Raising the Bar: "Cocktail Whisperer" Warren Bobrow Explains Why He Thinks Cannabis-Infused Cocktails Won't Be Just a Novelty', *Globe and Mail* (Toronto), 4 August 2018, p. 9.

6 Cooking with Cannabis

1 Robyn Griggs Lawrence, *Pot in Pans: A History of Eating Cannabis* (Lanham, MD, 2019), pp. 101–5.
2 Alia Volz, *Home Baked: My Mom, Marijuana, and the Stoning of San Francisco* (New York, 2020), p. 48.
3 Lester Grinspoon, *Marihuana Reconsidered: The Most Thorough Evaluation of the Benefits and Dangers of Cannabis*, 2nd edn (San Francisco, CA, 1994), p. 202.
4 John Rosevear, *Pot: A Handbook of Marihuana* (New York, 1967), pp. 77, 80.
5 Mahash Isyurhash and Garry Rusoff, *The Gourmet Guide to Grass* (New York, 1974), p. viii.
6 Hassan I. Sabbah, *Leaves of Grass* (Brighton, 1971).
7 Vera Rubin and Lambros Comitas, *Ganja in Jamaica: A Medical Anthropological Study of Chronic Marihuana Use* (The Hague, 1975), p. 50.
8 J. F. Burke, 'Eat It', *High Times*, 1 February 1978, pp. 47–9.
9 Elise McDonough, Marcus Nilsson and Ho-Mui Wong, *Bong Appétit: Mastering the Art of Cooking with Weed* (Los Angeles, CA, 2018), p. 4.
10 Michael Pollan, *The Botany of Desire: A Plant's-Eye View of the World* (New York, 2001), p. 150.
11 Interview with the author, 24 May 2023.
12 Chris S. Duvall, *The African Roots of Marijuana* (London, 2019), p. 220.

Select Bibliography

Abel, Ernest L., *A Comprehensive Guide to the Cannabis Literature* (Westport, CT, 1979)

Bobrow, Warren, *Cannabis Cocktails, Mocktails and Tonics* (Beverley, MA, 2016)

Borougerdi, Bradley J., *Commodifying Cannabis: A Cultural History of a Complex Plant in the Atlantic World* (Lanham, MD, 2018)

Campos, Isaac, *Home Grown: Marijuana and the Origins of Mexico's War on Drugs* (Chapel Hill, NC, 2012)

Clarke, Robert C., and Mark D. Merlin, *Cannabis: Evolution and Ethnobotany* (Berkeley, CA, 2013)

Dalotto, Todd, *The Hemp Cookbook: From Seed to Shining Seed* (Rochester, VT, 2000)

DeGrandpre, Richard, *The Cult of Pharmacology: How America Became the World's Most Troubled Drug Culture* (Durham, NC, 2006)

Dufton, Emily, *Grass Roots: The Rise and Fall and Rise of Marijuana in America* (New York, 2017)

Duvall, Chris, *Cannabis* (London, 2015)

Grinspoon, Peter, *Seeing through the Smoke: A Cannabis Specialist Untangles the Truth about Marijuana* (Essex, CT, 2023)

Guba, David A. Jr, *Taming Cannabis: Drugs and Empire in Nineteenth-Century France* (London, 2020)

Hart, Carl, *Drug Use for Grown-Ups: Chasing Liberty in the Land of Fear* (New York, 2021)

Kimmens, Andrew C., *Tales of Hashish: A Literary Look at the Hashish Experience* (New York, 1977)
Lawrence, Robyn Griggs, *Pot in Pans: A History of Eating Cannabis* (Lanham, MD, 2019)
McDonough, Elise, Marcus Nilsson and Ho-Mui Wong, *Bong Appétit: Mastering the Art of Cooking with Weed* (Los Angeles, CA, 2018)
Mills, James H., *Cannabis Britannica: Empire, Trade, and Prohibition* (Oxford, 2003)
Nance, Susan, *How the Arabian Nights Inspired the American Dream, 1790–1935* (Chapel Hill, NC, 2009)
Schivelbusch, Wolfgang, *Tastes of Paradise: A Social History of Spices, Stimulants, and Intoxicants* (New York, 1993)
Stoa, Ryan, *Craft Weed: Family Farming and the Future of the Marijuana Industry* (London, 2018)
Volz, Alia, *Home Baked: My Mom, Marijuana, and the Stoning of San Francisco* (New York, 2020)

Websites and Associations

The Antique Cannabis Book
www.antiquecannabisbook.com

The Cannigma
www.cannigma.com

Charlotte's Web
www.charlottesweb.com

Curiowellness
www.curiowellness.com

The Foggy Noggin' Diner
www.foggynoggindiner.com

Hash Marihuana & Hemp Museum
www.hashmuseum.com

Hempions
www.hempions.com

Hightimes
www.hightimes.com

Home Baked
www.aliavolz.com

Leafly
www.leafly.com

Leafwell
www.leafwell.com

Marijuana Moment
www.marijuanamoment.net

Ministry of Hemp
https://ministryofhemp.org

National Hemp Service
www.nationalhempservice.co.uk

Points
www.pointshistory.org

Weed Maps
www.weedmaps.com

Acknowledgements

Condensing so much cannabis history into such a short volume felt impossible, but it was accomplished thanks to the valuable help of some very important people. Michael Leaman provided excellent guidance and comments on the project, and Alex Ciobanu was so gracious as I navigated through all the weeds when narrowing down which illustrations to use. I couldn't have asked for a better picture editor. The same goes for Phoebe Colley, who applied her careful eye editing the text in such an invaluable way that I will forever be grateful. Nico Murillo was kind enough to allow me to visit her farm and talk about cannabis for an afternoon. Her culinary expertise has brought tremendous value to the project. I am also grateful to Tracee Tovanché, whose cooking skills were put to the test when I asked her for some recipes. She is an amazing special diet recipe developer. Tyler Gray agreed to lend his digital skills and photographic eye to help improve the illustrations, for which I am in his debt. The founder of Hempions, Fabian Braitsch, gave his time to converse with me about his hemp experiences, and Joshua Birchall deserves credit for lending me his ear and providing a recipe based on a traditional Brazilian sweet. I also want to thank Chris Duvall for sharing some valuable images and providing guidance whenever I reached out with questions. Andrew Garrett, the museum curator for the antique cannabis museum online, went out of his way to provide access to important material on the history of cannabis medicine, as did the folks at the Hash Marihuana & Hemp Museum in Amsterdam. I also want to thank the Special Collections Research Centre at the University of Kentucky Libraries for taking time to help me locate valuable materials. And to all my kinfolk out there who have talked cannabis with me over the years, thank you for lending your ears and your voices. I couldn't have done this without you.

This book would also not be possible if it weren't for my wonderful wife, Brandi, and our two incredible kids, Aiden and Meadow, for granting me the time needed to invest in this project. My life would not be same without their love and support.

Photo Acknowledgements

The author and publishers wish to express their thanks to the sources listed below for illustrative material and/or permission to reproduce it. Every effort has been made to contact copyright holders; should there be any we have been unable to reach or to whom inaccurate acknowledgements have been made, please contact the publishers and full adjustments will be made to any subsequent printings. Some locations of artworks are also given below, in the interest of brevity:

Ashmolean Museum, University of Oxford: p. 19; Bibliothèque nationale de France, Paris: pp. 9 (MS Latin 9474, fols. 88r and 90v), 76 (MS Français 2810, fol. 17r); courtesy Fabian Braitsch: p. 50; British Library, London: p. 99; courtesy Christopher Chabot, *High Times*: pp. 113, 114; collection of Chris Duvall: p. 117; Flickr: pp. 40 (photo Thomas Elliott, public domain), 86 (photo Mayra Chiachia, CC BY-SA 2.0), 101 (photo Tom Maisey, CC BY 2.0); courtesy Andrew Garrett, www.antiquecannabisbook.com: p. 103; Hash Marihuana & Hemp Museum, Amsterdam: pp. 61, 63, 94, 105 (photo Didier le Ger, CC BY-SA 3.0); iStock.com: pp. 33 (Marc Bruxelle), 36 (OpenRangeStock), 41 (SeaStock), 111 (Sarah Pender); courtesy Wonder Knack, www.wonderknack.com: p. 130; Library of Congress, Prints and Photographs Division, Washington, DC: pp. 30 (photo Dick DeMarsico), 97; Magnolia Pictures/Entertainment Pictures/Alamy Stock Photo: p. 122; The Metropolitan Museum of Art, New York: p. 68; courtesy Nico Murillo: pp. 65, 128; National Archives at College Park, MD: pp. 59, 83; National Portrait Gallery, Smithsonian Institution, Washington, DC: p. 77; courtesy Jonathan K. Nelson and Chris

Duvall: p. 15; The New York Public Library: pp. 25, 46; © 2018 David Oppenheimer – Performance Impressions Photography Archives: p. 123; PxHere: pp. 29, 32, 64, 72; from the *Report of the Indian Hemp Drugs Commission, 1893–94* (Shimla, 1894): p. 26; courtesy State Historical Society of Iowa, Iowa City: p. 56; from Cynthia Temple, *It Isn't All Right* (Boston and New York, 1861): p. 80; courtesy Tracee Tovanche: pp. 22, 52; Universiteit van Amsterdam: p. 12; University of Kentucky Libraries, Lexington (John Winston Coleman Jr Collection on Slavery in Kentucky): p. 24; Unsplash: pp. 6 (Margo Amala), 51 (K8), 90 and 107 (Elsa Olofsson); U.S. Drug Enforcement Administration: p. 73; U.S. Food and Drug Administration: p. 88; courtesy Alia Volz: pp. 119, 120; Wellcome Collection, London: p. 108; Wikimedia Commons: pp. 8 (photo Klaus Rassinger/Museum Wiesbaden, CC BY-SA 4.0), 17 (photo Караулов, CC BY-SA 4.0), 21 (photo Felix Bildstein, CC BY-SA 4.0), 43 (photo François Goglins, CC BY-SA 4.0), 57 (photo D-Kuru, CC BY-SA 3.0 AT), 84 (photo Roger McLassus, CC BY-SA 3.0), 89 (photo Stas2k, public domain), 91 (photo Trougnouf, CC BY 4.0), 110 (photo El Mono Español, CC BY-SA 4.0), 125 (photo Eli Christman, CC BY 2.0).

Index

italic numbers refer to illustrations; **bold** to recipes